CliffsNotes™
Investing in
401(k)s

By Scott Gilpatric

IN THIS BOOK

- Calculate how much money you need to save for a comfortable retirement

- Understanding how 401 (K) plans can help you achieve your retirement goals

- Choose the investments and risk level that are right for you

- Reinforce what you learn with CliffsNotes Review

- Find more Internet information about buying PCs in the CliffsNotes Resource Center and online at www.cliffsnotes.com

IDG BOOKS WORLDWIDE

IDG Books Worldwide, Inc.
An International Data Group Company
Foster City, CA • Chicago, IL • Indianapolis, IN • New York, NY

About the Author

Scott Gilpatric is a Ph.D. candidate in economics at Texas A & M University. He has published research in law and economics and has written numerous articles on economic issues for trade and educational publishers.

Publisher's Acknowledgments

Editorial

Project Editor: Tracy Barr
Acquisitions Editor: Mark Butler
Associate Acquisitions Editor: Karen Hansen
Technical Editor: J. Patrick Gorman

Production

Indexer: York Production Services, Inc.
Proofreader: York Production Services, Inc.
IDG Books Indianapolis Production Department

CliffsNotes™ Investing in 401(k)s
Published by
IDG Books Worldwide, Inc.
An International Data Group Company
919 E. Hillsdale Blvd.
Suite 400
Foster City, CA 94404
www.idgbooks.com (IDG Books Worldwide Web site)
www.cliffsnotes.com (CliffsNotes Web site)

Library of Congress Catalog Card No.: 99-66731
ISBN: 0-7645-8544-4
Printed in the United States of America
10 9 8 7 6 5 4 3 2 1
1O/QY/RS/ZZ/IN
Distributed in the United States by IDG Books Worldwide, Inc.
Distributed by CDG Books Canada Inc. for Canada; by Transworld Publishers Limited in the United Kingdom; by IDG Norge Books for Norway; by IDG Sweden Books for Sweden; by IDG Books Australia Publishing Corporation Pty. Ltd. for Australia and New Zealand; by TransQuest Publishers Pte Ltd. for Singapore, Malaysia, Thailand, Indonesia, and Hong Kong; by Gotop Information Inc. for Taiwan; by ICG Muse, Inc. for Japan; by Intersoft for South Africa; by Eyrolles for France; by International Thomson Publishing for Germany, Austria and Switzerland; by Distribuidora Cuspide for Argentina; by LR International for Brazil; by Galileo Libros for Chile; by Ediciones ZETA S.C.R. Ltda. for Peru; by WS Computer Publishing Corporation, Inc., for the Philippines; by Contemporanea de Ediciones for Venezuela; by Express Computer Distributors for the Caribbean and West Indies; by Micronesia Media Distributor, Inc. for Micronesia; by Chips Computadoras S.A. de C.V. for Mexico; by Editorial Norma de Panama S.A. for Panama; by American Bookshops for Finland.
For general information on IDG Books Worldwide's books in the U.S., please call our Consumer Customer Service department at **800-762-2974.** For reseller information, including discounts and premium sales, please call our Reseller Customer Service department at **800-434-3422.**
For information on where to purchase IDG Books Worldwide's books outside the U.S., please contact our International Sales department at 317-596-5530 or fax 317-596-5692.
For consumer information on foreign language translations, please contact our Customer Service department at **1-800-434-3422,** fax 317-596-5692, or e-mail rights@idgbooks.com.
For information on licensing foreign or domestic rights, please phone +1-650-655-3109.
For sales inquiries and special prices for bulk quantities, please contact our Sales department at 650-655-3200 or write to the address above.
For information on using IDG Books Worldwide's books in the classroom or for ordering examination copies, please contact our Educational Sales department at **800-434-2086** or fax 317-596-5499.
For press review copies, author interviews, or other publicity information, please contact our Public Relations department at **650-655-3000** or fax **650-655-3299.**
For authorization to photocopy items for corporate, personal, or educational use, please contact Copyright Clearance Center, 222 Rosewood Drive, Danvers, MA 01923, or fax **978-750-4470.**

Table of Contents

INTRODUCTION

You may have heard of 401(k) plans, either from your employer, a financial advisor, or a friend, but you may have questions about what they are, whether they're right for you, and how you go about investing in one. Or you may already know about 401(k) plans, but you want a better understanding of what these plans offer. In either case, this book is the place to find the answers to your questions.

A 401(k) plan is one of the best investment options available for retirement savings. Nearly all large firms offer a 401(k) plan to their employees today, and the number of smaller firms that offer 401(k) plans is large and growing all the time. The number of participants continues to grow because 401(k) plans offer tax advantages and flexibility that make them a great way save.

Why Do You Need This Book?

Can you answer yes to any of these questions?

- Do you need to learn about 401(k) plans fast?

- Do you not have time to read 500 pages on 401(k) plans?

- Does your employer offer a 401(k) plan, but you've hesitated to take part because you don't want your money locked away and don't understand how these plans work?

- Have you started to think about planning for your retirement but don't know where to turn for advice and guidance?

- Do you already contribute to a 401(k) plan but are concerned that you are not getting the most out of it?

If so, then CliffsNotes *Investing in 401(k)s* is for you!

How to Use This Book

You're the boss here. You get to decide how to read this book. You can read the book from cover to cover or just look for the information you want and put it back on the shelf for later. Here are a few ways you can search for your topics.

- Use the index in the back of the book to find what you're looking for.

- Flip through the book, looking for your topic in the running heads.

- Look for your topic in the Table of Contents in the front of the book.

- Look at the In This Chapter list at the beginning of each chapter.

- Look for additional information in the Resource Center or test your knowledge in the Review section.

- Flip through the book until you find what you're looking for — I organized the book in a logical, task-oriented way.

Also, to find important information quickly, you can look for icons strategically placed in the text:

If you see a Remember icon, make a mental note of this text — it's worth keeping in mind.

If you see a Tip icon, you know that you've run across a helpful hint, uncovered a secret, or received good advice.

The Warning icon alerts you to something that could be dangerous, requires special caution, or should be avoided.

Don't Miss Our Web Site

Keep up with the changing world of retirement investing and 401(k) plans by visiting the CliffsNotes Web site at www.cliffsnotes.com. Here's what you'll find:

- Interactive tools that are fun and informative
- Links to interesting Web sites
- Additional resources to help you continue your learning

At www.cliffsnotes.com, you can even register for a new feature called CliffsNotes Daily, which offers you newsletters on a variety of topics, delivered right to your e-mail inbox each business day.

If you haven't yet discovered the Internet and are wondering how to get online, pick up *Getting On the Internet*, new from CliffsNotes. You'll learn just what you need to make your online connection quickly and easily. See you at www.cliffsnotes.com!

CHAPTER 1

THE BASICS OF 401(K) PLANS

IN THIS CHAPTER

- Understanding what a 401(k) plan is
- Understanding how tax deferment works with a 401(k) plan
- 401(k) terms to know
- Knowing what features all 401(k) plan share

This chapter shows you the fundamentals of 401(k) plans: what they are, what purpose they serve, what makes them unique, and why you should care. Understanding these issues gets you closer to your ultimate goal — knowing how to use a 401(k) plan to maximize your retirement savings.

Investing a small amount of time to learn the concepts and terminology that define 401(k) plans pays off as you explore the details and make choices that best suit your needs. The tax benefits of a 401(k) plan make it an important investment opportunity that you don't want to miss.

The Purpose of the 401(k) Plan

A 401(k) plan is an individual investment account that employers offer to help their employees save for retirement.

- The money you put into a 401(k) plan is *tax deferred,* which means that the IRS doesn't consider this money as current income for tax purposes.

■ Tax deferment makes a 401(k) account an extremely efficient way to save by letting you sacrifice less of your income today and enjoy more in your retirement.

Table 1-1 illustrates that your bottom line income is greater if you invest in your company's 401(k) plan than if you don't.

Table 1-1: The Power of the Plan

	With a 401(k) Plan	Without a 401(k) Plan
Gross income	$35,000	$35,000
401(k) contribution	-$3,000	0
Taxable income	$32,000	$35,000
Standard deduction and personal exemption	-$4,250	-$4,250
Tax on $4,250 to $25,350 of income at 15% rate	-$3,165	-$3,165
Tax on remaining income at 28% rate	-$1,862	-$2,702
Total taxes paid	$5,027	$5,867
Net income (income after taxes)	$26,973	$29,133
Contribution ($3,000) growth at 10%	+$300***	N/A
Tax on growth ($300)	None (this is tax-deferred income)	N/A
Adjusted net income	$27,273 ($26,973 + $300)	$29,133
The amount you *control* after the first year	$30,273 (you still have your $3,000)	$29,133
Bottom line	After the first year, you would have $1,110 more than if you had not invested in your company's 401(k) plan.	

As you read Table 1-1, keep the following in mind:

■ The standard federal income tax personal exemption deduction for single people is $4,250 (for married couples filing jointly, it's $7,100).

■ Single taxable income on less than $25,350 is 15 percent; on $25,350 to $61,400, it's 28 percent (this last figure is known as your *marginal rate*).

For more information on your taxes, read *Taxes For Dummies*, 2000 Edition, by Eric Tyson, IDG Books Worldwide, Inc.

■ A 10 percent growth rate is arbitrary. Depending on the types of investments you opt for, your rate of return could be higher or lower.

Notice that if you invest through your 401(k) plan, in this example, you have an extra $1,120 each year to spend or save because of the tax savings. In addition, when you retire, you will have accumulated much more savings. The benefits of tax-deferred investing through your 401(k) plan are twofold:

■ First, because the money you save in 401(k) plan is tax deferred, you pay less tax on your annual income, leaving you with more money to either save or spend today.

■ Second, the money you save grows more quickly because the tax you would have paid on investment returns remains in your account to continue earning a return.

Defining a 401(k) Plan

You've probably heard a little bit about 401(k) plans, through reading an article in a financial magazine or by reading through the plan summary provide by your employer. And you may have found yourself confused or frustrated by some of the jargon that is used to describe what they are. For example, you've probably seen or heard the following terms:

- Retirement plan

- Cash or deferred arrangement, or *CODA*

- *Qualified* for tax deferment by employees and tax deductibility for employers

- *Defined contribution* rather than defined benefit plan

The following sections explain these terms and what they tell you about your 401(k) plan.

Retirement plan

A retirement plan is simply any plan operated by an employer or employee organization (such as a union) specifically for the purpose of providing income to employees when they retire. Retirement plans allow employees to defer (or hold off) a portion of their pay until retirement. When you save money in a 401(k), you are earmarking money for retirement and not for some other purpose like taking a trip around the world.

When you put money into a 401(k) plan, you are accepting a tradeoff. The IRS is offering you a tax break in exchange for your commitment to use the money for your retirement.

- You can break this commitment, but only at a financial cost to you (Chapter 8 examines the consequences of early withdrawal in detail).

- The penalties for withdrawing funds before you retire make 401(k) plans unsuited for other savings goals.

You may face substantial penalties for withdrawing funds from your 401(k) prior to retirement, so be sure to keep savings aside for other needs that will arise.

Cash or deferred arrangement (CODA)

This term describes the option of an employee to choose to receive some portion of his or her compensation from an employer as either a cash payment or a contribution to a 401(k) plan. So when you hear the term "CODA," just remember that all this means is that you have a choice of how to receive some of your salary. This distinguishes a 401(k) plan from other retirement plans such as pensions, which do not allow you, as the employee, such a choice.

Qualified

The word *qualified* is often used to describe a 401(k) plan — without stating explicitly what the plan is qualified for. *Qualified* simply means that a 401(k) plan is qualified under the Internal Revenue Code to allow the following:

- You, as the employee, to put off payment of taxes on contributions you make to the plan

- Employers to deduct payments into 401(k) plans from their taxes

Defined contribution rather than defined benefit

Retirement plans are classified as either *defined contribution* or *defined benefit* plans:

- **Defined benefit:** A pension is the typical defined benefit plan. Once you qualify for an employer's pension, you are promised a specific, or defined, pension payment each year of your retirement.

- **Defined contribution:** A 401(k) plan is a defined contribution plan. It does not promise any specific payment upon retirement. Instead, you specify the contributions you want to make into the plan throughout your career, and the total value of your account upon retirement will depend on the contributions you choose to make and your earnings from these investments.

Because a 401(k) plan is a defined contribution rather than defined benefit plan, what it will be worth when you retire depends on how much you contribute. A 401(k) plan is *not* a guaranteed retirement income.

What All 401(k) Plans Have in Common

Every 401(k) plan is designed by an employer specifically to suit the needs of his or her firm. If you work for a large corporation, your 401(k) plan is probably quite different from a 401(k) plan offered by a small firm. But all 401(k) plans have certain features in common.

Employer-provided

To participate in a 401(k) plan, your employer must offer it. If your employer offers a 401(k) plan, you will get two documents describing the plan:

- The *plan document*, which contains the fine-print, legal descriptions of all aspects of the plan

- The *summary plan description* (SPD), a more readable document that (ideally) summarizes the specific plan your employer offers

Professionally managed

The day-to-day management of investments is handled by your employer or, more commonly, an outside management organization, such as a mutual fund company, investment bank, or insurance company.

Take advantage of the fact that your 401(k) is professionally managed to save yourself the time and effort it takes to track the markets.

Voluntary, limited contributions

Because you make contributions to your 401(k) plan at your discretion, the contributions are *voluntary*. Contributions are also limited. The primary IRS limitation is a simple annual cap on your contributions; in 1998, the cap was $10,000. This cap is adjusted annually for inflation (in $500 increments).

The IRS has other, more complex restrictions on contributions, and your employer may establish limits as well. Chapter 3 covers these limits in detail.

401(k) Plans versus Traditional Pension Plans

Although employers may choose whether or not to offer a 401(k) plan and how to administer it, these plans differ from traditional employer pensions in many ways:

■ You choose whether to participate, and, although your employer may contribute matching funds (as Chapter 7 shows you), contributions to a 401(k) account come principally from you.

■ You retain much control over how the account is managed on your behalf.

■ The payoff when you retire depends on what you contribute throughout your career and the investment choices you make.

You will owe taxes on your initial contributions and the earnings of these investments when you withdraw them. And if you withdraw funds before retirement you may also face significant additional tax penalties (see Chapter 8 for a discussion of early withdrawals). This is why contributions to a 401(k) plan are said to be tax *deferred* rather than tax *free*.

401(k)s and Inflation

Many people rely solely on pension payments and social security to provide their retirement income. For the following reasons, that may not be the best choice:

■ Pensions are usually a fixed amount, and their purchasing power several years from now will decline based on the inflation rate.

■ Although Social Security currently has cost of living adjustments (COLAs), the program faces a funding crunch, and lawmakers have discussed eliminating the COLAs.

If you knew the rate of future inflation today, you could determine what the real value of your pension and Social Security benefits will be during your retirement years so that you could plan accordingly. However, the problem of inflation is made more serious by the fact that the inflation rate is unpredictable. The chart in Figure 1-1 shows the annual inflation rate in each year since 1945.

Figure 1-1: The inflation rate has varied significantly over time.

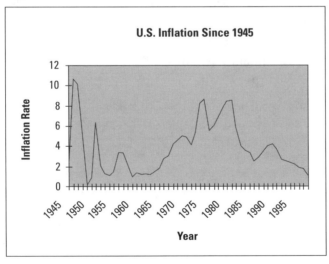

Table 1-2 illustrates how inflation impacts how much of your retirement income a fixed pension provides. And because inflation doesn't stop when you retire, the value of your pension will continue to decline.

Table 1-2:   Impact of Inflation on Fixed Retirement Income

Item	Scenario 1	Scenario 2
Planned annual retirement expenditures in today's dollars	$25,000	$25,000
Years until retirement	25	25
Average annual inflation rate between now and retirement	3%	6%
Dollars needed in first year of retirement to meet planned expenditures	$52,250	$107,250
Percentage of your retirement income provided by a $15,000 a year fixed pension	29%	14%

Remember

Investing through your 401(k) plan can insure you against the danger of inflation eroding the value of fixed retirement benefits.

CHAPTER 2
BENEFITS OF 401(K) PLANS

IN THIS CHAPTER

- Reducing your tax burden
- Watching your money grow more rapidly
- Being able to access your money in emergencies
- Investing easily

Even though you are convinced you need to be saving aggressively for your retirement, you may still have doubts about whether investing through your employer's 401(k) plans is the best way to do it. Maybe you are hesitant to commit a large share of your monthly income to a retirement plan that restricts access to your savings. Perhaps you don't expect to spend the rest of your career with your current employer and worry about what will happen to your savings when you quit. Or you may simply believe that you have better investment options that can provide a higher return than your 401(k) plan.

These are all important concerns, but they shouldn't stop you from investing in your 401(k) plan. The advantages of investing through your 401(k) plan are considerable, and, although your employer administers it, your 401(k) plan allows a surprising degree of individual choice, flexibility, and control.

Pay Less Tax

A 401(k) plan allows you to invest for retirement in a tax-deferred account. This means that the money your employer pays you that you put directly into your 401(k) plan is not treated as current taxable income. The earnings on your 401(k) investments are also not treated as current taxable income. Instead, you pay taxes on these earnings when you receive them in retirement (or if your withdraw them early).

If you're in a lower tax bracket when you retire

When you retire, you will probably be in a lower tax bracket because your primary salary will be gone, and your income from other sources such as pensions and investment earnings will be significantly less than your salary. If you hold off paying taxes on the part of your income that you put toward retirement savings, then when you do pay tax on these earnings (when you receive them as distribution from your 401(k) plan in retirement), you face a lower tax rate.

Table 2-1 illustrates how you might benefit if you face a 28 percent tax rate while working, and this rate falls to 15 percent when you retire (and assuming that you save $4,000 annually).

Table 2-1: Money You Can Save by Paying Taxes Later

	Non tax-deferred	Tax-deferred
Annual contribution to savings	$4,000	$4,000
Tax rate	28%	15%
Taxes paid on annual contribution	$1,120	$600
Total taxes on 35 years of savings	$39,200	$21,000
Total tax savings		$18,200

The total tax you have to pay depends on what your annual income will be in retirement and what the tax rates will be at that time.

You might wonder, "What if the tax rate I have to pay goes up by the time I retire?" It is true that this could happen, either because the government significantly increases income tax rates or because, between now and your retirement, your financial position becomes much better.

If you're in a better financial position when you retire, you really don't have anything to be concerned about. If your income in retirement is greater than it is presently, then you should be better able to afford the tax costs than you are today, so deferring taxes will have served to allow you to pay them when you are in a stronger financial position.

However, despite the fact that it may feel as though the government is constantly raising taxes, in fact, marginal income tax rates have largely held steady or fallen for the last couple decades.

Other tax deductions

A final tax benefit of investing in your 401(k) plan is that by reducing your adjusted gross income, you may then be eligible for other tax deductions. For example, you can deduct major medical expenses (those in excess of 7.5 percent of your adjusted gross income) from your taxes. If you have a lower adjusted gross income due to 401(k) plan investing, you will be eligible to deduct more of the expense if such a case arises.

Watch Your Savings Grows More Rapidly

In addition to reducing your taxable income, tax-deferred investing enables your savings to grow more rapidly, resulting in a much greater accumulated savings when you retire.

The best way to appreciate the benefits that a 401(k) plan offers you is to compare investing in a 401(k) plan with investing through a private brokerage. Figure 2-1 illustrates the advantage a 401(k) plan gives you over private investing (assuming both get a 10 percent annual return on your investments).

Figure 2-1:   With tax-deferred investing, your savings grows more quickly.

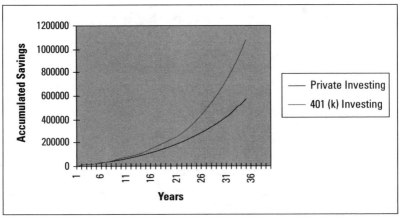

Why the big difference? When you invest through your 401(k) plan, the money you would have paid in tax on your investment earnings stays in your account and earns additional interest. Another benefit of saving through your 401(k) plan is that you also have more after-tax income each year you work. Table 2-2 shows where a $40,000 annual salary goes in both private investing and 401(k) investing.

Table 2-2:   Private Investing vs. 401(k) Investing

	Private Investing	401(k) Investing
Annual income	$40,000	$40,000
Savings	$4,000	$4,000
Taxable income	$40,000	$36,000
Annual tax	$7,950	$6,830
Income after tax and savings	$28,050	$29,170

Keep in mind when you read this table that the annual tax is computed based on a 15 percent tax rate on first $25,000 of income and 28 percent tax rate on remaining taxable income.

Enjoy Plan Flexibility

The tax advantages of 401(k) plans are the primary reason to use them as a tool for retirement saving, but, as noted at the beginning of this chapter, many people worry about committing money into the hands of their employer for a distant future retirement. The benefits of 401(k) investing certainly do come with a trade-off: when you contribute to your 401(k) plan, you accept certain restrictions on access to your money. But 401(k) plans offer quite a bit of flexibility that should reduce your concerns:

- **You control how much you contribute into your 401(k) account from each paycheck.** If you find yourself facing unexpected expenses one month, you can reduce your contribution to help meet these costs. In this respect, 401(k) plans are quite different from some other employer-provided retirement plans like pensions, which require that a portion of your compensation go to your retirement and don't allow you the option of receiving the money immediately as cash during a difficult period.

Occasionally, transaction fees may be associated with changing or skipping your monthly contribution; be sure to investigate your 401k plan's policy for hidden fees.

- **You decide how to invest your savings.** Most 401(k) plans offer many investment choices with varying levels of risk. Although the plan is administered by your employer, who typically hires outside fund managers, you choose which broad classes of assets to invest your money in.

- **The money in your 401(k) plan is yours, not your employer's.** Unlike a pension that you lose if you leave your employer before it is vested, the money you contribute to your 401(k) plan stays with you. Although there may be vesting requirements for employer matching contributions, as explained in Chapter 8, you face no loss due to changing jobs or layoff.

- **You can access your 401(k) savings in times of need.** Although you face penalties for early withdrawals in some cases, many plans offer hardship withdrawals without penalty in case of an event such as a major illness. For other financial demands of a less severe nature, you may be able to borrow against the value of your account. These features are discussed in Chapter 9.

Invest Effortlessly

Many people fail to maximize the return they receive on their investments or fail to invest at all simply because they find it difficult and time consuming. But investing in a 401(k) plan is simple for the following reasons:

Automatic withdrawal of contributions

This means you never even have to write a check. You can specify to your employer how much you would like to contribute each month and how you would like it to be invested. Your employer takes it from there.

Employer administration of funds

Because your employer administers your 401(k) plan, you face less paperwork than you would if you invested privately. Furthermore, if you have questions about your plan, want to make changes in how your money is invested, or want to take a loan against the value of your plan, you usually can do so simply by speaking to the plan administrator at your workplace. This is often more convenient than finding time to sit down with a banker or investment broker.

Professional investment management

Making the most of your investments requires that they adjust to changing market conditions. When you invest through your 401(k), you don't need to spend your time seeking out stock tips or reading financial pages in order to ensure you invest wisely. The professionals that manage the funds in which you invest perform this function, although you may still want to study which funds perform best. You also will probably save on commissions and other trading costs compared to private investing because you will benefit from pooling your funds with many others who participate in your employer's plan.

Take advantage of the simplicity of 401(k) investing. Often people fail to save simply because after the money is in their hands they find a reason to spend it. When 401(k) contributions are directly withheld from your salary, it ensures that you won't divert planned retirement saving to other spending.

CHAPTER 3
ASSESSING YOUR INCOME AND SAVINGS PLAN

IN THIS CHAPTER

- Determining your current financial position
- Understanding your present and future financial obligations
- Determining whether you're prepared to meet your obligations

Armed with a basic understanding of the role of a 401(k) plan in retirement planning, you're ready to start the crucial work of determining how you can use this important tool to your advantage. The first step is gaining an understanding of your current financial position and knowing what position you want to be in when you retire.

You might say, "Right now, I don't have enough money; my goal is to have plenty by the time I retire." Of course planning for your retirement isn't quite that simple. In order to begin effectively planning for retirement, you have to know your current net worth and how you spend what you earn. And you have to examine all your financial goals and obligations and understand what meeting them will take. These are the first steps in financial planning.

Remember

You make financial decisions every day, and, if you don't have a plan to guide you, reaching your destination will take much longer — if you are lucky enough get there at all.

Calculating Your Current Financial Position

Two measures describe the state of your finances:

- *Net worth:* Your net worth is simply a measure of what you have: the value of your assets minus the value of your debts. Net worth measures where you stand right now.

- *Net saving:* Unlike net worth, which you can measure at any moment in time, you must evaluate net saving over some period, say one month. It measures your income minus your expenditures over that time. In other words, net saving measures which direction you are going and how fast.

Calculating your net worth and net saving is worth the time it takes so you know where you stand.

The following sections tell you how to determine your net worth and your net saving.

Your net worth: assets and debts

Determining your net worth is a simple accounting exercise, but it sometimes provides surprising results. For example, you may have debts spread out over so many different credit cards and other loans that you've lost track of how much you owe. Or you may find that your assets are greater than you thought, but they are concentrated in areas that aren't providing much of a return.

To figure out your net worth, you first need to calculate your assets. Fill out the worksheet shown in Table 3-1 to determine your assets. List all of your assets and their current value — that is, not what you paid for them nor what you hope they will be worth ten years from now, but what they are worth today. These are some typical assets you may have:

■ Ready cash and deposits such as checking accounts, savings accounts, money market funds, certificates of deposit (CDs), and just plain cash

■ Investments such as government bonds, bills, and notes, corporate stocks and bonds, mutual funds, cash value of life insurance policies, and real estate

■ Tangible assets, such as your home, automobiles, boats, jewelry, antiques, artwork, and home furnishings

You can approximate; you don't have to have your house and cars appraised unless you really want an exact figure.

Table 3-1:   Assets Worksheet

Types of Asset	Value
Ready cash and deposits (checking and savings accounts, money market funds, etc.)	$
Investments (government bonds, corporate stocks and bonds, mutual funds, cash value of life insurance policies, etc.)	$
Tangible assets (your home, for example), automobiles, boats, jewelry, antiques, home furnishings, etc.	$
Your business or your share in a partnership	$
Deferred assets (401(k) plan, IRAs, annuities, etc.)	$
Total value of all assets	$

After you calculate the value of your assets, use the worksheet in Table 3-2 to figure out your liabilities (debt). Listing all your liabilities may be painful, but being honest with yourself is the first step toward improving your situation. These are some typical liabilities you may have:

- Mortgage and home equity loans, as well as other debts related to your home such as property taxes or home improvement loans

- Loans for major purchases, such as automobiles and home furnishings

- Student loans

- Credit card debt, including major credit cards as well as department store cards and gas cards

Table 3-2:   Liabilities Worksheet

Types of Liabilities	Value
Mortgage and home equity loan balances plus other home-related debts (property taxes, home improvement loans, etc.)	$
Loans for major purchases (cars, furniture, etc.)	$
Student loans	$
Credit card debt (major credit cards, store cards, gas cards, etc.)	$
Debt to the IRS for taxes	$
Total Liabilities	$

When you complete the both the Assets and Liabilities Worksheets, you can determine your net worth by subtracting your total liabilities from your total assets.

If you're just beginning your career and your net worth is small — or even negative — don't despair. It's not unusual that debts such as student loans or a new mortgage are much greater than any assets you may yet have. Time is on your side, and the fact that you are already thinking about investing in your 401(k) plan means that you probably will be able to prepare well for your retirement.

If you're closer to retirement and find that you have little or no net worth, you are in a more difficult situation. You have to make trade-offs between saving heavily in the remaining years of your career, planning to delay your retirement, reducing your income expectations during your retirement, and perhaps working part-time when retired.

Your net saving: income and expenditures

Most of us know precisely how much we earn each month from our employer. But do you know how much you spend each month and where the money goes, or how much you typically earn on your investments? If not, now is the time to remedy that. To determine your net saving, grab another sheet of paper and divide it into two columns: income and expenses (see Table 3-3).

First, list all sources of income on the left. On the Income column, in addition to your after-tax salary, be sure to include any of the following that apply:

- Interest on your checking, savings, and money market accounts

- Approximate monthly return on investments, such as bonds or mutual funds

  Leave out earnings on deferred retirement accounts such as your 401(k) or IRAs.

- Alimony or child support

After you list your income, list your expenses. Some expenses — like mortgage payments — are obvious. But others aren't so obvious. To figure out what to include in your budget, pull out your old check logs and credit or debit card statements and put all your entries into categories. Those categories are the ones you need to include in your budget. You would include the following items, for example, when you identify your expenses:

- Mortgage or rent and property taxes and home maintenance

- Utilities

- Insurance premiums

- Groceries and household goods

- Auto expenses (fuel, maintenance, and repair)

- Interest on loans

- Eating out and entertainment

- Clothing

- Commuting and other work-related expenses

- Personal expenses: haircuts, massages, health club membership

- Educational expenses and child care

- Alimony, child support, and so on

- Charitable donations

To get a monthly estimate for items like travel, find what you spent over the past year and divide that amount by twelve.

Table 3-3: Income and Expenditures Worksheet

Sources of Income	Average Monthly Value	Categories of Spending	Average Monthly Expense
Salary or wages after taxes	$	Mortgage or rent and other home expenses	$ $
Interest on your checking, savings, and money market accounts	$ $	Utilities (including phone, cable TV, cellular, and internet service)	$
Approximate return on investments, such as bonds or mutual funds.	$	Groceries and household goods	$
Alimony or child support	$	All insurance costs	$
Other	$	Clothing and personal expenses	$
		Eating out, entertainment and travel	$
		Interest on loans including credit card, student and auto debts	$
		Gas and auto expenses	$
		Child care, child support, eldercare, schooling, pet care	$
		Other	$
Total Income	**$**	**Total Spending**	**$**

When you complete the worksheet, follow these steps to determine your net saving:

1. Add up your total monthly income.

2. Add up all your expenses.

3. Subtract your expense from your total income.

The resulting figure is your net saving.

Your Present and Future Obligations

In order to have a complete sense of your financial position, you need to know your financial obligations and goals as well as your current resources. Of course, because this book concerns 401(k) plans, it is primarily focused on retirement planning. It is important, however, that as you plan for retirement, you keep in mind other demands on your financial resources and how they can affect your ability to save for retirement.

Setting a retirement goal

A critical part of retirement planning is setting a specific goal. You need to put a figure on your desired annual retirement income in today's dollars. (Chapter 4 explains how much total savings you'll need when you retire in order to meet your goal.)

If you've already calculated your current monthly income and expenditures (see the preceding section), estimating a reasonable retirement income is relatively easy. Professional financial planners often advise that you should plan to meet *at least* 75 percent of your pre-retirement expenses — ideally 80 percent or more. If you're many years from retirement, use the 75-80 percent rule to estimate your needed retirement income. For example, if you currently spend about $50,000 per year, plan to have a retirement income of about $40,000.

If you're close enough to retirement that you've started to make specific plans for your retirement years, you need to make a more specific forecast of your expenses during retirement:

1. Adjust for the changes that come with retirement.

2. Estimate the annual cost of fulfilling your plans.

3. Add this amount to the annualized expenditures you calculated earlier.

If you are 15 years from retirement, for example, and your monthly expenses are $4,000, your annual retirement budget may look like the one in Table 3-4. This sample assumes the following:

■ The mortgage is paid off and the kids' college is paid for, saving you an additional $14,000.

■ Your medical expenses increase by 2,000 per year.

■ You plan to spend every summer during your retirement taking a major trip, which you expect to cost around $4,000.

Table 3-4:   Example Annual Retirement Spending

Item	Amount
Current monthly expenses	$4,000
Current yearly expense	$48,000 (4,000 x 12 months)
Minus savings due to being retired	- $14,000 (mortgage and tuition expenses gone)
Plus added expenses of aging and retirement	+ $6,000 (medical expenses + yearly travel)
Annual retirement spending goal	$40,000

This amount is in current dollars. Chapter 4 explains how to put a figure on the total savings you'll need to meet your annual income goal.

If you are still young and many years from retirement, your goal may change several times as your income, expenses, and other life circumstances change. It is nevertheless smart to start thinking now about what you want your income to be in retirement so that you can see what you have to do to reach your goal.

Other savings goals

You probably have more immediate financial goals than retirement that require a portion of your savings. Plan for these as well so that they don't derail your retirement plans. What these goals are depends on what stage of life you're in. Following are just a few examples of what might affect you between now and your retirement:

■ Purchasing a home

■ Sending kids to college

■ Starting your own business

Don't let your retirement plans be jeopardized by failing to plan for other needs.

Unexpected expenses

Many people are unable to save as much as they plan to because they find themselves reacting to a string of unexpected obstacles like major car and household repairs, accidents, or perhaps job loss or layoff. If you can anticipate and prepare for "unexpected" events, these type of expenses need not divert funds intended for retirement saving.

To be prepared for the major curves life throws you, try to have a rainy day savings fund equal to about two months of expenses, if possible. This is a significant amount of money, but it can save you from having your plans completely dashed by an unfortunate turn of events.

You don't need to have all your rainy day money in an instantly accessible investment, like a savings account, that earns a poor return. By investing a portion in a bond fund or a stock fund that holds relatively low risk stocks, you can earn a substantially better return without unreasonable risk or lack of liquidity.

Don't let retirement saving be forgotten until it's too late because other needs seem more urgent. In addition to setting aside money for rainy day expenses and other financial needs, be sure to save for retirement throughout your career.

Assessing Your Readiness to Meet Your Obligations

The key to building your net worth and reaching all your financial goals is saving and investing wisely. The following sections offer suggestions on ways you can improve your ability to meet your short-and long-term financial goals.

All successful financial planning starts by living within your means. To save adequately for your retirement and other obligations, you probably need to save 10 to 20 percent of your income.

Evaluate current investments

If you've already accumulated a significant net worth, address whether your assets are invested in a way that earns a good return and best helps you reach your financial goals. Consider the following examples:

- If you're close enough to retirement that other major goals are behind you, you may want to take full advantage of tax-deferred retirement investing opportunities such as your 401(k) plan. If you've been putting your savings into a non-tax-deferred mutual fund, for example, you could probably do much better by simply investing in a similar type of fund through your 401(k) plan because of the tax advantages.

- Ask yourself whether your current investments are well diversified. If not, you could probably achieve a similar return with less risk by diversifying your portfolio.

- If, to maintain liquidity and avoid risk, you've kept a large proportion of your assets in certificates of deposit or a money market account that have low returns, you may want to consider whether earning a higher return in exchange for less liquidity and somewhat more risk might not be a worthwhile trade-off.

Evaluate current savings

Take a hard look at how you are spending your income and what you can change to make room for greater saving. Sometimes little things can make a big difference. Breaking the habit of having a $4 latte or cappuccino everyday can free up more than $1,000 annually for saving.

Evaluate current debt

Try to pay off (or down) your credit card balances. One of the most common financial traps people find themselves in is having large credit card balances that incur a high rate of interest. Table 3-5 shows how much the same money would make if you could invest it in a 401(k) plan.

Table 3-5:   401(k) versus Credit Card Interest

	With $10,000 Credit Card Debt	With 401(k) Plan
What you do with $200 per month	Pay the interest on your debt	Purchase investments such as stocks
Total contributed years	$48,000	$48,000 over 20
What you have at the end of the period	$10,000 debt remaining (you've only paid interest)	$121,000 for retirement (assuming 8% annual return)

Tip

If you are saddled with significant credit card debt, what should you do? Following are a few strategies you can try to lower — or eliminate — this debt:

- Many card issuers now offer rates as low as 9.9 percent on credit card debt to those with a good credit record. Call the banks that issue your cards and ask them for a lower rate.

- Check out a credit card consolidation loan or transfer your balances to a new account at a lower rate.

- Make your top priority paying off the accounts with the highest rates first. No investment can compete with the return you'll get by paying off loans that charge upwards of 18 percent interest.

CHAPTER 4

DETERMINING YOUR ANNUAL 401(K) PLAN CONTRIBUTION

IN THIS CHAPTER:

- Knowing what you can expect from Social Security
- Knowing how much your pension will provide after inflation
- Figuring out how much you need to save before retirement
- Figuring out how much you need to contribute
- Understanding 401(k) contribution limits

After you determine your net worth and how much money you need each year in retirement (as explained in Chapter 3), you can figure out exactly what meeting your annual retirement income goal will take. To do so, you need to see how much of your income Social Security and your pension (if you have one) can be expected to provide, and then you have to determine how much you need to save to close the gap between this and your retirement income goal.

What to Expect from Social Security

For most people, Social Security provides an important component of retirement income, but you should not be under the impression that Social Security alone will be sufficient for a comfortable retirement. How much you can expect to receive from Social Security when you retire depends on your income throughout your career. If your retirement is less than 20 years away, you can complete and submit a Social Security Statement of Estimated Benefits form to get an estimate of the benefits you will receive, based on your work history. You can get this form at the Social Security Web site, http://www.ssa.gov/ssa-7004 or from your local Social Security office, or call 1-800-772-1213.

If you haven't yet had a very long work history or you are content with a rough estimate of what you will receive, use Table 4-1 to determine approximately how much Social Security you will receive annually in retirement.

Table 4-1: Approximate Social Security Benefits

Average Annual Earnings throughout Career	Approximate Annual Benefit
$10,000-$20,000	$7,000
$20,000-$30,000	$9,000
$30,000-$40,000	$11,000
$40,000-$50,000	$12,500
$50,000-$60,000	$13,500
$60,000+	$14,500

Remember: For Table 4-1, figures for average annual earnings and annual benefits are in today's dollars.

Social Security alone will not provide adequately for your retirement. It is up to you to save to meet your goal.

What You Need at Retirement

Use the Annual Unmet Retirement Income Worksheet in Table 4-2 to calculate your annual unmet retirement income goal. (You can find your inflation adjustment factor in Table 4-3.)

Remember

By the time you retire, because of inflation, you will need *more* income in order to achieve the standard of living you want.

Table 4-2:   Annual Unmet Retirement Income Worksheet

	Mary	*Your Numbers*
1. Enter retirement income goal	$40,000	$
2. Subtract annual Social Security benefit (from Table 4-1)	-$13,500	$
3. Subtract pension benefit if COLA is included	-$0	$
Remaining income needed in today's dollars	=$26,500	$
4. Multiply by inflation adjustment factor (from Table 4-3) *2.81		
Inflation-adjusted income need	=$74,465	$
5. Subtract pension benefit without COLA	-$10,000	$
Total: Annual unmet retirement income in future dollars	=$64,465	$

The example supposes that Mary has a retirement income goal of $40,000. When she retires, her average annual income over her career will have been about $50,000, so she expects to receive $13,500 from Social Security. She will also get a $10,000 per year pension, but it does not have a guaranteed COLA.

Table 4-3: Inflation Adjustment Factor

Years to Retirement	Inflation Adjustment Factor	Years to Retirement	Inflation Adjustment Factor
1	1.03	21	1.86
2	1.06	22	1.92
3	1.09	23	1.97
4	1.13	24	2.03
5	1.16	25	2.09
6	1.19	26	2.16
7	1.23	27	2.22
8	1.27	28	2.29
9	1.30	29	2.36
10	1.34	30	2.43
11	1.38	31	2.50
12	1.43	32	2.58
13	1.47	33	2.65
14	1.51	34	2.73
15	1.56	35	2.81
16	1.60	36	2.90
17	1.65	37	2.99
18	1.70	38	3.07
19	1.75	39	3.17
20	1.81	40	3.26

Perhaps you are left with a much larger unmet need than you expected, either because Social Security doesn't provide what you thought or your pension isn't worth as much after adjusting for inflation as you believed. This is a very common situation to face. The good news is that your 401(k) plan offers a great way to close the gap.

How Much You Need to Contribute

How much savings you need to achieve your goal depends in part on how long a retirement you want to plan for. If you plan on retiring at 65 and expect to live to 85, you have 20 years of retirement, for example. If you hope to retire at 60 and want to be sure you will have enough to last until you are 95, you have to plan for a 35 year retirement. Even if you don't yet know what kind of retirement to plan for, this exercise can help you understand the implications of different plans for your savings needs. To determine what you need to save annually to meet your retirement goal, complete each of the worksheets in the following sections.

Calculate your total retirement savings goal

To calculate your total requirement savings goal, follow these steps:

1. Find your savings multiplier from Table 4-4 by locating the row that indicates the length of retirement you're planning for and choosing one of the annual return percentages. This number is your multiplier.

2. Enter the multiplier in the appropriate place in the Total Savings Needed for Retirement Worksheet (see Table 4-5).

3. Multiply this number by your unmet annual retirement income goal (from Table 4-2).

Table 4-4: Savings Multiplier

Length of Retirement	6% Annual Return	8% Annual Return	10% Annual Return
20 years	15.4	13.1	11.4
25 years	18.0	14.8	12.5

(continued)

Table 4-4: Savings Multiplier *(continued)*

Length of Retirement	6% Annual Return	8% Annual Return	10% Annual Return
30 years	20.2	16.2	13.3
35 years	22.2	17.2	13.9
40 years	23.9	18.1	14.3

In the example, Mary plans for a 20-year retirement and uses an 8 percent annual return.)

Table 4-5: Total Savings Needed for Retirement Worksheet

	Mary	Your Calculations
1. Enter the annual unmet retirement income goal (refer to Table 4-2)	$64,465	$
2. Enter and multiply by the savings multiplier (refer to Table 4-4)	*13.1	
Total savings needed for retirement	$844,492	$

The product is how much you need to save by the time you retire to meet your annual goal. This is your total retirement savings goal.

Remember

The return on your investments after you retire makes a substantial difference in how much you must save for retirement. If you find this surprising, remember that you will continue to earn a significant amount of money on your investments after you retire. The higher the return, the slower you will draw down your principle savings, especially in the early years of retirement. Figure 4-1 shows how the value of your savings will decline over a 25 year retirement for two cases, both of which provide $25,000 annual income, but one case assumes a 6 percent annual return, the other a 10 percent return.

Figure 4-1:   A 10 percent return allows a much smaller initial savings to provide for a 25 year retirement than if investments return 6 percent.

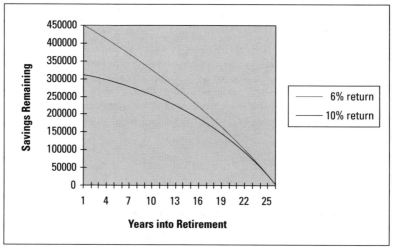

So what return should you plan on getting after retirement? Although planning on a 10 percent return on investments during your career is reasonable, you probably want to lower this to an 8 percent return after retirement because you'll want to reduce your exposure to market risk. On the other hand, if you are confident that your basic needs will be met in retirement and are willing to take a little greater risk in the hope of enjoying more income, a 10 percent return may be appropriate.

Calculate your annual contribution

After you know your total retirement savings goal, you can calculate what you have to do to get there. The first step is to know how much you already have (refer to Chapter 3 for a discussion on net worth). Following are some assets that can contribute to your retirement:

■ The money you have already saved in your 401(k) plan, IRA, or other investments that are not earmarked for another purpose (like a college fund)

■ Other assets, such as the equity in your home

To determine how your current assets can figure toward your retirement, follow these steps:

1. Enter the present value of your assets in the Estimated Value of Assets Worksheet (see Table 4-6).

2. Using Table 4-7, find your asset appreciation multiplier and enter it into the Estimated Value of Assets Worksheet.

3. Multiply the present value of your assets by the asset appreciation multiplier.

Table 4-6:   Estimated Value of Assets Worksheet

Example	Your calculations
1. Enter present value of assets $10,000	
2. Enter multiplier from Table 3-6 25.55	
Estimated value of your assets when you retire	$255,500

In the example, Mary has assets worth $10,000 already saved for retirement and multiplies this by 25.55, the multiplier corresponding to 35 years and a 10 percent annual return.

Table 4-7: Asset Appreciation Multiplier

Years until Retirement	8% Return	10% Return	Years until Retirement	8% Return	10% Return
1	1.00	1.00	21	4.66	6.73
2	1.08	1.10	22	5.03	7.40
3	1.17	1.21	23	5.44	8.14
4	1.26	1.33	24	5.87	8.95
5	1.36	1.46	25	6.34	9.85
6	1.47	1.61	26	6.85	10.83
7	1.59	1.77	27	7.40	11.92
8	1.71	1.95	28	7.99	13.11
9	1.85	2.14	29	8.63	14.42
10	2.00	2.36	30	9.32	15.86
11	2.16	2.59	31	10.06	17.45
12	2.33	2.85	32	10.87	19.19
13	2.52	3.14	33	11.74	21.11
14	2.72	3.45	34	12.68	23.23

Table 4-7: Asset Appreciation Multiplier

Years until Retirement	8% Return	10% Return	Years until Retirement	8% Return	10% Return
15	2.94	3.80	35	13.69	25.55
16	3.17	4.18	36	14.79	28.10
17	3.43	4.59	37	15.97	30.91
18	3.70	5.05	38	17.25	34.00
19	4.00	5.56	39	18.63	37.40
20	4.32	6.12	40	20.12	41.14

To calculate the additional saving you'll need to meet your retirement goal, follow these steps:

1. Using the Additional Savings Needed Worksheet (shown in Table 4-8), enter the total savings needed for retirement (from Table 4-2).

2. Subtract the value of your assets (from Table 4-6).

Table 4-8:   Additional Savings Needed Worksheet

	Example	Your calculations
1. Enter total savings needed for retirement from Table 4-2	$844,492	$
2. Subtract value of assets at retirement from Table 4-6	-$255,500	$
Additional savings needed	**$588,992**	**$**

Figuring your annual contributions

The annual contributions required to reach your goal depend on how many years you have until you retire and on the rate of return that you base your plans on. To determine your annual contributions, follow these steps:

1. Using the Annual Contribution Worksheet (in Table 4-9), enter the how much additional savings you need from Table 4-8.

2. Find your annual contribution multiplier from Table 4-10 and enter it in the appropriate line in the Annual Contribution Worksheet.

3. Multiply the additional savings you need by the annual contribution multiplier.

Table 4-9: Annual Contribution Worksheet

	Example	Your calculations
Enter additional savings needed from Table 4-4	$588,992	$
Enter multiplier from Table 4-10	*.004	$
Annual contribution	**$2,356**	**$**

For example, Mary multiplies $588,992 by .004 (because she has 35 years until retirement and plans on a 10 percent average return) and finds that she needs to contribute $2,356 each year to achieve her retirement goal.

Table 4–10:　Annual Contribution Multiplier

Years until Retirement	8% Return	10% Return	Years until Retirement	8% Return	10% Return
1	1.000	1.000	21	.020	.016
2	.481	.476	22	.018	.014
3	.308	.302	23	.016	.013
4	.222	.215	24	.015	.011
5	.170	.164	25	.014	.010
6	.136	.130	26	.013	.009
7	.112	.105	27	.011	.008
8	.094	.087	28	.010	.007
9	.080	.074	29	.010	.007
10	.069	.063	30	.009	.006
11	.060	.054	31	.008	.005
12	.053	.047	32	.007	.005
13	.047	.041	33	.007	.004

Table 4-10: Annual Contribution Multiplier

Years until Retirement	8% Return	10% Return	Years until Retirement	8% Return	10% Return
14	.041	.036	34	.006	.004
15	.037	.031	35	.006	.004
16	.033	.028	36	.005	.003
17	.030	.025	37	.005	.003
18	.027	.022	38	.005	.003
19	.024	.020	39	.004	.002
20	.022	.017	40	.004	.002

The Limits on 401(k) contributions

As mentioned in Chapter 1, several rules limit annual 401(k) contributions:

■ The most basic is a flat cap of $10,000 annually on each person's pre-tax contributions (this amount is adjusted annually for inflation).

■ You and your employer together cannot contribute more than $30,000 or 25 percent of your annual compensation, whichever is less. Check with your plan administrator if you think you might encounter this limit.

■ If you earn over $80,000 annually, you may have contributions limited to as little as 6 or 8 percent of your salary. If you fall into this category, talk to your plan administrator or human resources staff to find out what limits you will encounter.

If you run up against a limit on how much you can contribute to your 401(k) plan, the next best place to turn is usually an IRA. With an IRA, you can also shield investment earnings and sometimes contributions from taxes.

What to Do If You Come Up Short

If the annual contribution you calculated is much greater and beyond your ability to save, you can do one of the following:

■ If you've been choosing a conservative return on investments throughout your calculations, be a bit more aggressive in your investment plans. Keep in mind that this means some added risk.

- Revise your planned date of retirement. Retiring two or three years later can make a big difference because it gives you more time to save, reduces the amount you need to accumulate, and may increase your annual Social Security benefit.

- Think about other resources you can draw on for retirement that you haven't already included, such as some inheritance you're likely to receive between now and retirement.

If the annual contribution you've calculated seems unreasonable, you need to consider whether you want to change your retirement plans or change your spending and saving habits today.

CHAPTER 5
UNDERSTANDING YOUR INVESTMENT OPTIONS

IN THIS CHAPTER:

■ Understanding risk and how it affects you

■ Knowing what investment options are available in most 401(k) plans

When you spend less than you earn, you are saving, but *investing* is something different. When you invest, you put your savings into any of a great many types of assets in the expectation of earning a positive return over time. Unlike company pensions that treat all employees alike, most 401(k) plans offer a large variety of investment choices. Typically, when you invest through your 401(k) plan, you don't directly purchase bonds or shares in individual companies. Instead, you purchase shares through *mutual funds* (or simply *funds)* that hold many different *securities* belonging to a particular class. (A security is simply a claim of ownership of a financial asset and usually refers to stocks or bonds.) For example, an equity fund holds shares in perhaps hundreds of different firms on behalf of thousand of investors (like you) who, in turn, own a share of the fund.

The specific 401(k) plan your employer offers determines exactly how you can invest the money you contribute. To take advantage of a 401(k) plan, you must know your options, how much risk each involves, and how to choose among them.

Any time you invest your money in an asset that does not offer a complete guarantee of what your investment will be worth in the future, there is some risk. In other words, *all* investments involve some risk, although the type and degree of risk varies greatly across different classes of assets. This chapter contains the basic information you need in order to understand the risks and benefits of each broad class of investment and to know which investments make sense for you.

Money Market and Bond Funds

Fixed income funds, such as money market and bond funds, are funds that invest in instruments that promise a fixed return (known as the *yield)* until a specified date (the *maturity* date), at which the time the principal is repaid. What differentiates one fund of this type from another is the securities in which it invests. Table 5-1 shows a comparison of the different types of government funds.

Table 5-1: **Government Bonds**

Type of Fund	Description	Risk	Return
Government money market	Invests only in U.S. treasury securities that mature within one year or, most commonly, within a few days	Little risk	Very low
Intermediate government bond funds	Invest in U.S. treasury bonds that mature in 5-10 years	Greater risk; return may be eroded due to inflation	Higher than money market, on average
Long-term government bond funds	Invest in U.S. treasury bonds that mature after more than 10 years	Same as preceding; also more exposed to market risk	Higher still

Remember

Government bonds offer a guaranteed return, but they are subject to inflation risk.

Corporate bonds are similar to government bonds except that the guarantee of interest and repayment of principle is made by a corporation rather than the government. The same types of risk apply, with the added factor of *credit risk*, the risk associated with the possibility that the corporation may default on its debts. Even for major corporations, this risk is not insignificant, especially over long periods such as twenty years. Consequently, corporate bonds pay a higher return than government bonds.

Guaranteed Investment Contracts

A *guaranteed investment contract* (GIC) is a contract between a corporate retirement plan, such as your 401(k) plan, and an insurance company. The retirement plan invests money with the insurance company, which promises to pay interest at a fixed rate over the specified life of the contract. The insurance company then invests the money in the expectation of earning a higher return than the interest it pays.

GICs are a very popular investment option with many 401(k) plan participants:

- They offer guaranteed income and thus relatively little risk.

- They typically pay a higher return than other fixed-income alternatives like money market accounts and some bond funds.

Investing in a GIC does involve some credit risk associated with the possibility the insurance company will default. However, in most cases, this risk is probably very small, and GICs do offer a low risk investment alternative.

GICs carry little risk but achieve a lower return than stocks in the long run. Still, if you're near retirement, want to avoid risk, and, at the same time, earn a better return than you can get on such assets as money market funds, GICs may be a useful option.

Common Stocks

An important part of every 401(k) plan participant's portfolio is investments in *common stocks*, also known as *equities*. When you own stock in a company, you own a share of that corporation.

Stocks have two great advantages that make them a key asset when investing for retirement:

- Stocks offer greater insurance against inflation than fixed-income assets, such as bonds.

- Over the long term (at least ten years), the return on equities most likely will be greater than on other classes of assets.

Of course, the drawback is that when you invest in stocks, you are exposed to significant market risk. Particularly in the short run, this risk is a major concern unless you have enough money invested that you can absorb a major loss if the market crashes. The level of risk differs, of course, depending on the type of stocks you purchase — shares in Ford and GE carry less risk than shares in small internet firms, for example.

If you work for a large firm, you may have literally dozens of stock funds to choose from, which vary according to things like the size of the firms they invest in and the investment strategies followed by the funds' managers. Table 5-2 lists and briefly describes some of the terms used to describe stock funds.

Table 5-2: Types of Equity (Stock) Funds

Type of Fund	Description
Stock index funds ("passively managed" funds)	Invest in the firms that make up such well-known stock indices as the Standard and Poor 500 index. Rather than try to beat the market, these funds simply seek to mirror it.
Actively managed funds	Funds' managers try to earn a better return than the market as a whole; most do not.
Large capitalization funds ("large cap funds)	Invest only in large firms, typically those firms whose traded stock is worth at least $5 billion. Such shares typically carry less risk than shares in smaller firms, but the average return over time is also lower.
Small and medium capitalization funds	Invest in firms averaging under $2 billion market capitalization (for small caps) and $2-5 billion (medium caps). Smaller firms generally have better growth prospects and offer a higher prospective return, but the risk is greater.
Income funds	Invest in relatively mature firms whose shares pay above average dividends. Relatively low risk and low return.
Growth funds	Invest in firms expected to grow at a rapid pace. Relatively high risk and possible return.
Aggressive growth funds	Focus on small firms that have the prospect of particularly rapid growth but also of sudden collapse. Tend to do very well at times and very poorly at others but offer a high payoff in the long term.
Global, international, and foreign stock funds	Invest at least a large share of their funds outside the U.S. The risk associated with investing in these funds depends on what types of shares they hold and in what countries. All foreign investments have some additional risk due to the possibility of fluctuations in international exchange rates.

Stocks offer the best inflation protection and long run return, but they carry significant short run market risk.

Employee Stock Ownership Plans (ESOPs)

In an ESOP, you invest a significant part of your savings in shares of the company for which you work. Doing so lets you participate in a very direct way in your own company's financial success (or failure).

Although you may have good reasons to participate in an ESOP, remember that investing a large share of your savings in your own company leaves your asset portfolio undiversified and exposes you to specific risk. If your company takes a turn for the worse, you could suddenly find your own financial future turning bleak. Even if you think your firm has a great future, limit your exposure by investing only a reasonably small portion of your retirement savings in your ESOP.

Is participating in your companies ESOP a good idea? The incentives your employer provides may very well make this a good prospective investment, particularly if, as an employee with direct experience of the company's inner workings, you are confident that it has a very strong financial future. However, use caution when investing a large share of your savings in your own company because it leaves your asset portfolio undiversified. If your company takes a turn for the worse, you could suddenly find your own financial future turning bleak. The fact that your own career and future earnings are tied to the same company makes investing solely in ESOPs even more dangerous; you could conceivably both loose your job and much of your investments.

If you invest too much in an ESOP, you can be heavily exposed to loss in the event of a downturn in your firm's fortunes. Refer to Chapter 7 for information about types of risk.

Mixed (or Balanced) Funds

Balanced funds invest in a combination of stocks and bonds. A skilled fund manager may be able to shift assets to stocks when the stock market is rising and shift them to bonds when a downturn in stocks seems likely. These funds typically involve less market risk than investing solely in stocks, while at the same time offering reasonable protection against inflation risk; however, they average a lower return than equities in the long term.

Keeping Track of What Your 401(k) Plan Offers

To help you keep track of the investment options that your 401(k) plan offers, use the checklist in Table 5-3.

All investments carry risk, but not all risks are equal. You should now have the knowledge to understand the risks associated with different types of investments. This is the key to making informed choices that reflect your own financial situation and goals.

Table 5-3:   401(k) Investment Options

Option	Offered? Y/N	Notes
Government bonds		
Money market		
Intermediate government bonds		
Long-term government bonds		
Corporate bonds		
Guaranteed investment contract		
Common Stocks		
Stock index funds		
Actively managed funds		
Large cap funds		
Small and medium cap funds		
Income funds		
Growth funds		
Aggressive growth funds		
Global, international, and foreign stock funds		
ESOP		
Mixed (or Balanced) Funds		

Other Retirement Savings Plan Options

401(k) plans are not the only tax-advantaged retirement savings option. Of course this book is focused on 401(k) plans, but it is worth a few moments to become aware of other retirement savings vehicles that may also help you invest more effectively.

Individual Retirement Accounts

You've probably heard of *Individual Retirement Accounts* or *IRAs*. Like 401(k) plans, IRAs are a vehicle through which you can save for retirement in a tax-deferred manner. IRAs differ from 401(k)s in the following ways:

- **IRAs are not offered by employers.** You can open an IRA at a bank, brokerage, or other financial institution and invest in almost any type of financial assets.

- **Initial contributions may or may not be tax-deductible.** Like a 401(k) plan, taxes on earnings from money invested in an IRA are deferred until withdrawn at retirement, but whether your contributions are deductible depends on the type of IRA you choose (there is a wide variety) and for which you are eligible. Generally, if you are eligible to contribute to a 401(k) plan and your income is over $40,000 ($60,000 if married), you're not be eligible for a tax-deductible IRA, although you may contribute to a non-deductible IRA.

- **Tax-deductible contributions to IRAs are treated slightly differently than 401(k) contributions:** Rather than directly reducing your adjusted gross income as 401(k) contributions do, deductible IRA contributions allow you to deduct the amount of the contribution when you file your taxes. This means that you will not receive the refund for the tax until you file your return, whereas 401(k) contributions immediately reduce the tax deducted from you salary.

- **Contributions to IRAs are capped much lower than 401(k) contributions at $2000 annually.**

A 401(k) plan is usually a better option than an IRA for tax-deferred retirement investing, but there are a couple of cases in which an IRA can be very useful:

- **If you leave your employer.** You can rollover the money in your 401(k) account into an IRA and continue earning a tax-deferred return. (For more about this see Chapter 9.)

- **If you want to save more than the maximum allowed annual contribution to your 401(k) plan.** A Roth IRA is often the best way to save additional money for retirement.

SEPs, Keoghs, and so on

You may have heard of 403(b) Plans, Keoghs, and SEPs. They are other retirement savings plans. However, if you are eligible for a 401(k) plan, you are almost certainly not eligible for these.

- A *403(b)* plan is nearly identical to a 401(k) plan except that it is offered by non-profit institutions such as hospitals, publics school systems, and universities. If you are eligible for a 403(b), nearly everything in this book should apply equally to your plan, but you may want to check with your plan administrator if you have any question.

- A *Keogh* is a tax-deferred retirement plan available to self-employed individuals. If you or your spouse is self-employed, you may want to learn more about whether this option can benefit you.

- *Simplified Employee Pensions,* or *SEPS,* are also generally used by those who are self-employed or work for several different employers throughout the year. They are very similar to IRAs but allow employer contributions.

CHAPTER 6
INVESTING SUCCESSFULLY FOR RETIREMENT

IN THIS CHAPTER

■ Principles for successful investing

■ Investing at different stages in your life

■ Sample investment strategies

Investing is about making choices. One of the advantages of investing through a 401(k) plan is that 401(k) plans are typically professionally managed. You don't need to spend a lot of time and effort tracking the markets, examining the performance of individual firms in which you hold stock, or monitoring your investments on a daily basis. What you *do* need to do is understand what types of investments make sense for you, given your goals, time-horizons, and tolerance for risk.

Basic Principles for Successful Investing

You can spend a great deal of time studying investment strategies and learning the latest hot tips, but you probably either don't want to do that or don't have the time. Fortunately you don't need to. Following these simple rules ensures that you save and invest effectively to create wealth for your retirement goal.

Because saving and investing for retirement should begin as early in your career as possible, giving you many years to save, retirement investing has a *long time horizon.* A long time horizon means that, over the years, the swings (market ups and downs) inherent in relatively risky investments balance out. With a long time horizon:

■ You can invest more aggressively in your 401(k) with assets — such as stocks — that carry greater risk but provide a better average return.

■ Funds earmarked for retirement need not be as *liquid,* or quickly accessible, as money saved for more immediate needs.

Set a goal and know what it will take to reach it

Before you can even begin to invest your money wisely, you have to have the discipline to save so that you have money to invest. Setting a goal and knowing what reaching that goal takes is important in achieving the discipline you need to make the sacrifices necessary to save sufficiently for retirement and other needs.

Start saving early

Whatever your retirement goal, begin saving as early as you can. Doing so enables you to spread the sacrifice over a longer period of time. For example, if you want to put $160,000 of contributions into your 401(k) plan over your career, contributing $4,000 annually over 40 years is a lot less painful than contributing $8,000 annually for 20 years.

The earlier you save, the more money you will have accumulated when you retire (see Table 6-1). The first column indicates the age at which saving begins, and the second column shows the accumulated balance at age 65, given annual contributions of $4,000 since saving began and an 8 percent annual return on balances.

Table 6-1:   Accumulated Savings Over Time

Age When Saving Begins	Accumulated Savings at Age 65
25	$1,123,124
30	$748,408
35	$493,383
40	$319,817
45	$201,691
50	$121,297
55	$66,581
60	$29,343

The reason saving and investing early make such a difference is that you benefit from the compounding of returns on your investments over a much longer time period. In other words, the $4,000 you invested when you were 25 will be worth $4,320 when you're 26, $4,665 when you're 27, and so on. As long as this money remains invested, the returns keep compounding.

Remember

Starting to save for retirement early in your career greatly reduces the amount you have to contribute yearly to reach your goal.

Utilize tax-deferred investment options like a 401(k) plan

When you invest through your 401(k) plan (or other tax-deferred retirement vehicle), you are accepting significant limitations on your ability to access your money in a pinch.

If you do find yourself needing to do so you may incur significantly penalties. The benefits of tax-deferment come at the cost of liquidity. Is this trade-off worth it?

The answer is yes. As Chapter 3 discusses, it is important to save for more immediate needs than retirement, such as your children's college education and rainy days, through more accessible investments that are not tax-deferred. However, you should designate a significant part of your savings for retirement and take advantage of tax deferral opportunities. For retirement investing, the benefits of tax-deferment greatly exceed the cost of reduced liquidity.

Understand that investing always involves risk

Investing always involves making decisions that balance risk and return. Although different individuals have different preference for risk and knowing your own tolerance is important, investing only in low risk assets may not be a good strategy for long term retirement planning.

Investing in stocks, for example, has more risk than investing in, say, government bonds. If you invest in bonds over 20 years, you can be quite confident that you'll receive the return you expect, perhaps 5 percent annually. If you invest in stocks, you're much less certain of the average annual returns over 20 years. Perhaps you expect a 10 percent annual return on your investment, but the actual return may very well turn out to be only 6 percent or may be as much as 15 percent.

However, the probability that you will receive a smaller return if you invest your retirement savings in stocks over 20 years than if you invest in government bonds is very, very small. The past century has had no 20-year period over which broad stock indices have under-performed government bonds.

Figure 6-1 shows the performance over twenty years of a bond that pays 5 percent annually and a stock fund with an expected return of 7.5 percent return. The performance of the stock fund is much more erratic (it carries greater risk), but over the long run, it performs better.

Figure 6-1: Over the long run, stocks generally out perform bonds.

If you avoid assets that offer a high average return in order to reduce your risk, you will either have to reduce your planned retirement income or save much more to achieve your goal.

Diversify your assets

The single piece of advice that financial advisors give most often is *diversify* your assets. When they say this, they are most commonly referring to equity investments, meaning that you should avoiding holding stock in just one or a few firms; instead you should invest in many different firms. But diversifying in other ways may also be wise. Consider these examples:

■ You might want to consider holding not just stocks but
   other types of assets such as corporate and government
   bonds.

■ Investing through different fund management firms
   enables you to diversify among financial managers
   (although doing so may involve higher fees).

Diversifying assets reduces risk without lowering expected
returns.

The reason owning several different assets of the same type,
rather than a larger share of one, is beneficial is that it enables
you to earn an equal average return with lower risk. An example illustrates why. Suppose you have $1,000 to invest
and can choose between two firms or invest $500 in each.
Assume that each firm has identical payoff probabilities.
If you invest all your money in one firm, your *expected return*
(the mean value among the distribution of possible outcomes) is 10 percent, yielding $1,100. But you have an equal
chance of having a payoff of $1,000 (0 percent return),
$1,100 (10 percent return), or $1,200 (20 percent return),
as shown in Figure 6-2.

Figure 6-2:   By investing in one stock, you're just as
                   likely to get a high, mid, or low payoff.

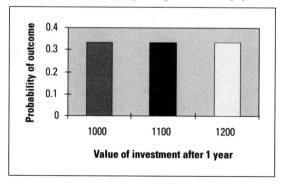

If you split your investment between the two firms, your expected return will be the same, 10 percent. But the probability that you will end up with either no return (0 percent) or a high return of 20 percent is reduced from 1/3 to 1/9 (because the chance of either of these outcomes is 1/3 x 1/3=1/9). See Figure 6-3.

Figure 6-3:   Diversifying lets you increases the likelihood that you'll receive a payoff near the mean.

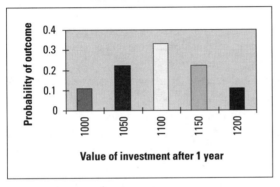

When you diversify, you want to invest in assets whose returns are not highly *correlated*, meaning they don't tend to rise or fall together. The performance of investments in Microsoft and Intel, for example, may be significantly correlated because they both depend heavily on demand for computers. When investing in stocks, the gains from diversification arise from the fact that if one firm does poorly, it has little effect on the performance of another firm.

But even returns on firms as different as a software developer and a public utility may be somewhat correlated because they both are effected by changes in the market for all stocks. That is, both benefit from a "bull" stock market, and both suffer in a "bear" market. For this reason, you may also want to reduce the risk of your investment portfolio by diversifying among asset classes such as by investing part of your savings in corporate and government bonds rather than shares.

Change your portfolio as your circumstances change

The right investments for you five years from now may be different from what is best for you today. People and their financial circumstances change over time, and your investment plan should change, too.

Part of modifying your investment plans over the years is simply adjusting to different stages in life. For example, if your net worth or income suddenly becomes much greater due to career advancement, inheritance, or even a booming housing market where you live, you may become more optimistic about your retirement. Whereas before you may have been primarily concerned with ensuring adequate income in your later years, now you may want to shoot for building a nest egg large enough to permit you to retire to Hawaii. In this case, you might decide to invest your savings more aggressively than you had been.

You should also change your investment portfolio if your investments perform poorly in the long run. In particular, if you choose to invest in actively managed funds that seek to beat the market, monitor whether they actually do so. If not, consider changing funds.

The performance of retirement investments should be measured over the long term — months and years, not days or weeks. Changing investment funds every time you hear of new high-flying fund doesn't make sense, and fees may be associated with doing so.

Investing Throughout Your Life

As you go through life, your income, obligations, and ability to tolerate financial risk will change. Your investments should change accordingly. Of course, each individual's life follows a unique path, but most of us follow common patterns as we age.

The early years

If you are just starting out your career — in your twenties, say, and not yet married or supporting children — you have significant advantages and disadvantages as an investor. Table 6-2 lists the things you have going for you and against you as an investor.

Table 6-2: Issues for the Young Investor

Advantages	Challenges
Your financial obligations to others are probably small or non-existent	Your income and net worth are both probably fairly low
You have far more freedom to spend your money as you like	You may have significant debts, such as student loans
You can afford to take risks with your investments because your obligations are small and you have many years to recover from losses	You may have substantial expense when starting out, such as the purchase of a car or furniture
	You still need to develop a savings fund to deal with life's emergencies

Because of the long time horizon for retirement investments at this age and because of your limited obligations, consider taking substantial risks with your investments. For example, you may want to concentrate on small cap stocks with high growth prospects and perhaps even equities in developing countries.

Middle years (30s and 40s)

As you start to have major obligations through marriage and child rearing, you financial circumstance certainly change. Table 6-3 lists the challenges and advantages you face as an investor.

Table 6-3:   Issues for the Middle Years Investor

Advantages	Challenges
Your income may now be significantly higher, especially if you are married and both you and your spouse work	Saving for retirement has to compete with saving for your children's college education and perhaps the purchase of a home
	Your expenses are higher

With the obligations that life brings, you probably want to reduce the risk of your investment portfolio compared to when you were young. However, reducing your risk does not mean you should avoid equities. You may want to add some fixed income assets to your investment mix, but you also need to hedge against the risk of inflation and continue to achieve significant growth. You may best be able to accomplish this by shifting assets into lower risk equities, such as large cap stock funds.

Be careful not to allow other demands on your resources to crowd out retirement savings too heavily during these middle years. If you don't contribute much to your retirement plan during this time, catching up in your later years will be very difficult.

As you near retirement (50s and early 60s)

The later years of your career will probably be the time when you are able to save the most. At this time in life, you should be saving a large share of your income so that you can continue to enjoy a good lifestyle once you retire. Table 6-4 shows the challenges and advantages you face.

Table 6-4: Issues for the Older Investor

Advantages	*Challenges*
If you are fortunate, many of your obligations will be reduced — children will be independent and your home mortgage paid off	Your investment time horizon is significantly shorter
Income is likely to be greater than ever before	

By this time in your life, your investment time horizon is considerably shorter. In order to ensure that your investments hold their value and provide adequately for your retirement, you may want to shift toward more fixed income securities. (Reducing your investment risk may be less of a concern if you've been able to save effectively throughout life and have accumulated a large net worth, in which case you may feel comfortable with greater risk exposure.)

Remember

Your ability to tolerate risk will probably decline as you age, so adjust your portfolio accordingly. See Chapter 7 for more information about risk.

UNDERSTANDING RISK

IN THIS CHAPTER:

- Knowing what part risk plays in investing
- Understanding the different types of risk
- Determining your own tolerance for risk

All investments involve some risk, although the type and degree of risk varies greatly across different classes of assets. As an investor choosing between different types of assets, you will face a fundamental tradeoff between lower risk and greater return: the more risk, the greater the return *on average* — but the greater the possibility of a large loss, as well.

Understanding the Types of Risk

One of the decisions you face when investing is what type of risk to accept. Fixed-income investments, such as bond funds, tend to leave you relatively exposed to inflation risk, whereas assets, such as stocks, offer much greater protection against inflation but carry greater market risk. Rather than fear risk, you need to understand the risks involved in each type of investment and whether these risks make sense for you, given your goals and circumstances.

Remember

All investments carry risk. Know the risks associated with your investments and how much risk is right for you.

Inflation risk

Inflation risk is the uncertainty about the real value of the return on an investment because of inflation. For example, some assets, such as government bonds, promise a fixed return with very little chance that the issuer will default. If you invest in these types of assets, you can be confident that you'll receive the promised return on your investment. What is far less certain is what the real value of these investments will be after you adjust for inflation.

Suppose, for example, that you purchase a bond for $1,000 that pays 8 percent interest annually for thirty years. Figure 7-1 shows what the real value of the investment will be (in today's dollars) after 30 years for different average rates of inflation over the period. Notice that a difference of only two or three percentage points in the inflation rate over a long period of time has a great impact on the value of such an investment.

Figure 7-1:   Inflation's effect on investment return.

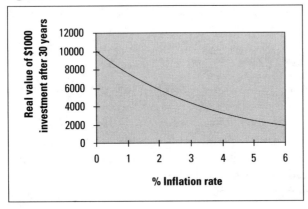

For long term investing, which includes all retirement investments until you are within 5 to 10 years of retirement, inflation risk is a very significant concern. Don't make the mistake of thinking that your investments carry very little risk because they offer a guaranteed return; this return may not be worth much after inflation. "Safe" investments like bonds may leave you exposed to inflation risk.

Market risk

Market risk is what most people have in mind when they talk about the risks of investing. This term usually applies to stocks and refers to the risk that the value of all stocks in the market will fall.

Market risk is a much greater factor in the short term than over a long period. For example, it is entirely possible that the market will fall and cause the value of your stocks to drop by 10 percent or more very suddenly. Even over periods of a few years, you may find that a bad market leaves you with little or no return on equity investments. However, when investing over periods of ten years or more, good years will very likely more than make up for bad years, leaving you with a strong return on equity investments.

Market risk is of much less concern when investing for the long term than in the short run.

Specific risk

When you invest in a particular firm, whether by purchasing its stock or bonds, you are exposing yourself to the risk that this specific firm performs poorly.

- The risk that the firm's stock falls in value is called *business risk*

- The risk that a firm defaults on its debt (such as bonds) is called *credit risk.*

Both business risk and credit risk are a type of *specific risk,* meaning that it is risk associated with investing in a single or a few firms rather than the entire market.

You also incur some specific risk if you invest in several firms in the same industry — say several computer makers. In this case, you face the risk that the computer industry as a whole will enter hard times.

With the investment funds that are typically available through your 401(k) plan, you can easily minimize your exposure to specific risk by investing in funds that hold a well-diversified portfolio of stocks, bonds, or whatever.

The one instance where you are likely to face specific risk is if you participate in an employee share ownership plan (ESOP). See Chapter 5 for more details on your investment options.

You can reduce specific risk by holding more diverse assets.

Determining Your Personal Tolerance for Risk

Although the stages of life and other factors have a similar effect on your ability to bear risk, don't forget that there is a personal component as well. You may be following a standard investment plan for a person at your point in life, but if you're loosing sleep worrying about whether the stock market will crash, you are probably taking on too much risk in your investments.

To determine how much risk is right for you, fill out the Risk Assessment Worksheet shown in Table 7-1. Remember, there are no right or wrong answers.

Table 7-1:   Risk Assessment Worksheet

Question	Answer	
1. Which of the following best describes you:	**a)** Your principal retirement goal is to ensure that you have an adequate income for a secure retirement. **b)** You'd prefer to strive for a more comfortable retirement with more to spend on fun but with the possibility that you will instead end up with insufficient funds to retire when you planned and therefore have to continue working longer. **c)** You'd really like to retire in grand style, and you are willing to incur a chance of loosing a significant part of your savings.	1.
2. Which would you prefer?	**a)** Set aside 20% of your income annually throughout your career in return for a guaranteed comfortable retirement. **b)** Set aside 15% of your income annually in return for 90% chance of a comfortable retirement and 10% chance that you'll be on a tight budget when you retire. **c)** Set aside 10% of your income annually in return for an 85% chance of a comfortable retirement, 10% chance the things will be tight financially, and 5% chance that you'll need financial support.	2.
3. What do you consider most important when investing?	**a)** Sure and steady returns **b)** Above average returns **c)** A chance at very rapid growth	3.
4. If you were given a choice betweenthe following, which would you choose?	**a)** $5000 cash **b)** a 50% chance at winning $15,000 **c)** a 10% chance at winning $500,000	4.
5. How would you characterize	**a)** Conservative, risk-averse	

yourself as an investor?   **b)** Moderately willing to take risks
                              c) Aggressive, a risk-taker
                                        5.

To figure out your score, give yourself 1 point for each A response, 2 points for each B response, and 3 points for each C response. Based on how many points you have, use the following scale to assess your attitude toward risk:

■ 5-8 points: You are a relatively conservative, risk-averse investor.

■ 9-12 points: You are a moderate risk taker.

■ 13-15 points: You are an aggressive, risk-seeking investor.

The following section offers a couple of sample investment choices that illustrate conservative and aggressive plans.

Sample 401(k) Plan Investment Choices Based on Risk Tolerance

This section looks at a couple of examples of how you might choose to invest your 401(k) plan savings over time, depending on the level of risk you're comfortable with. The first scenario shows a sample investment plan for an individual who is willing to invest fairly aggressively in order to achieve high growth prospects. The second scenario shows an investment plan for a person who is less comfortable with risk.

An aggressive investment plan

Figure 7-2 indicates a relatively aggressive investment mix at various stages of life.

Figure 7-2: A fairly aggressive investment plan.

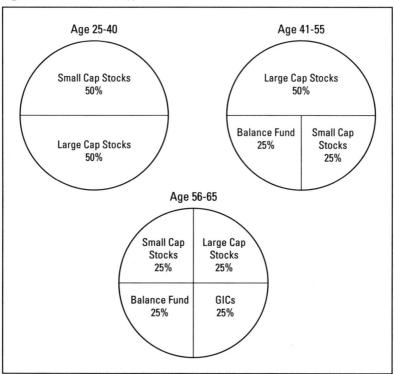

This aggressive investor holds primarily equities throughout his career, shifting a portion of his funds into government bonds (through the balanced fund) and GIC as retirement approaches.

A conservative investment plan

Figure 7-3 shows investment choices that a conservative investor might make.

Figure 7-3: A conservative investment plan.

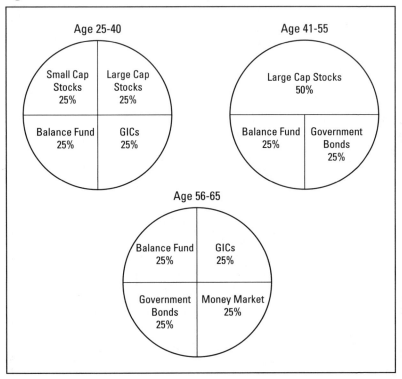

In Figure 7-3, the investor holds a large share of equities during most of his or her career to avoid inflation risk but concentrates more on lower risk large cap stocks than does the aggressive investor. As retirement nears, the conservative investor holds primarily fixed-income bonds, money market funds, and GICs.

CHAPTER 8
FEATURES DETERMINED BY YOUR EMPLOYER

IN THIS CHAPTER:

- Employer matching of contributions
- Rules for eligibility and vesting
- Valuation and why it matters
- The investment options available to you
- Rules on accessing your savings

Although all 401(k) plans have much in common, there are important differences between plans, based on the features and rules your employer chooses to include. What features your plan offers and how it is administered usually depend on the size of the firm you work for. Others features may depend on the role your employer sees for itself as a partner in helping you achieve a comfortable retirement.

Your employer should have documents that clearly explain the features of your plan. Take the time to familiarize yourself with these so you know what to expect from your 401(k) plan. (For information about these documents, refer to Chapter 1.)

Employer Matching of Contributions

Your 401(k) plan may have an *employer match* of contributions. If so, when you put money into your 401(k) plan, your employer makes a contribution as well. For instance, your employer may match contributions at $.50 on the dollar for contributions up to $5,000 annually. So if you contribute $4,000 this year, your employer would contribute an additional $2,000. Although the majority of 401(k) plans offer some type of matching of contributions, they vary widely in both the matching rate and the limit to how much may be contributed each year with the benefit of matching.

Funds contributed to your 401(k) plan by your employer are treated for tax purposes just like those you contribute yourself:

■ These contributions are almost always made pre-tax, and the earnings are tax-deferred just like all 401(k) earnings.

■ You generally only pay taxes on these contributions when you withdraw your savings after retirement.

Table 8-1 shows the value of annual matching funds at retirement, assuming 25 years of contributions earning an 8 percent return annually. If you fail to take part in a 401(k) plan with matching contributions, you are, in essence, turning down this money.

Table 8-1: The Value Of Matching Contributions

Annual match	$2,000	$3,000	$4,000
Total value at retirement	$159,908	$239,863	$319,817

If your employer does offer matching contributions, make the most of it! If you don't, you are literally choosing to be paid less than you are offered. And, if your 401(k) contributions are matched, it is a safe bet that no other investment will offer a return that is nearly as great.

Eligibility Requirements

Most firms that offer a 401(k) plan make all full-time employees eligible to participate (and part-time employees are eligible as well in some cases). However, many employers restrict eligibility based on the following:

- **Time on the job:** Many employers require that you work for the firm for some period — typically one year — before you can participate in a 401(k) plan.

- **Age of employee:** Many employers also restrict eligibility to those employees who are at least 21 years old.

Your employer may also have separate rules regarding eligibility for matching of contributions. For example, all employees may be eligible to participate in the 401(k) plan but only those who have worked for the firm for a year or more will receive matching funds. Check with your employer's Human Resources department to determine the rules at your firm.

Vesting

You may be familiar with the concept of *vesting* from experience with a traditional pension. A *vesting period* is a time during which an asset, such as a retirement benefit, does not belong entirely to you and may be lost under specific circumstances such as termination of employment.

The concept of vesting in 401(k) plans *applies only to contributions made by your employer.* When you contribute a portion of your compensation to your 401(k) plan, it is yours. Any money your employer contributes into your 401(k) account, however, may be subject to vesting requirements (in fact, two-thirds of firms having vesting requirements). Table 8-2 describes the two common types of vesting rules.

Table 8-2: Vesting Rules

Cliff Vesting	Graded Vesting
None of the money contributed by your employer belongs to you until you have been employed for a certain period of time.	With each year of service, you vest (or own) an increasing share of employer contributions to your 401(k) account.
If you leave before vesting date, you do not receive any of your employer's contributions, but after this date, employer contributions are 100% yours.	A five-year vesting rule may specify that, after the completion of each year of employment, you become vested for an additional 20 percent so that, at the end of five years, you are 100 percent vested.
The law specifies that the period of service required for cliff vesting cannot be greater than five years.	A graded vesting plan cannot exceed seven years.

In 401(k) plans, vesting requirements apply only to contributions made by your employer. After you are fully vested, all additional employer contributions belong to you from the moment they enter your account.

If you are not sure of the eligibility or vesting rules of your 401(k) plan, check your plan document or ask the plan administrator.

Before leaving your employer, be sure you are aware of rules for vesting and employer contributions. You certainly would like to avoid leaving just before employer contributions become vested. Also, some employers deposit matching contributions quarterly or semiannually. Staying on a few extra weeks may be worth it, if doing so means receiving significant matching funds for your 401(k).

Valuation

The value of the assets in your 401(k) account is constantly changing. If you own stocks, for example, everyday some will rise in value, and some will fall. Reconciling the value of your account to all these changes is called *valuation*. What differs among plans is the frequency with which valuation occurs.

■ The valuation frequency of 401(k) plans varies from annually to daily, but most plans are valued at least quarterly, and there is a marked trend toward daily valuation.

■ You can transact business on your account, such as changing the mix of your investments or cashing out of the plan, only when the plan is valued (or, in some cases, based on the most recent valuation).

■ More frequent valuation generally works to your advantage because you don't have to wait as long to make changes to your plan, to withdrawal money, or to have additional assets against which to borrow.

■ Daily valuation is more costly to administer than quarterly valuation. These administrative costs may be partially passed on to employee 401(k) accounts by your employer.

Investment Options

Your employer determines the individual investment funds that are available to you. Although in the past, 401(k) plans were sometimes set up to invest in a single asset, such as the company's own stock, today even the most limited plans typically offer at least three classes of assets. (See Chapter 5 for details on investment options.)

How many investment options are available to you generally depends on how large your firm is:

■ Typically, a large firm offers a much greater array of investment choices. Participants often can choose from a great variety of stock, bond, and mixed asset funds offered by different investment firms.

■ A small firm, on the other hand — one with fewer than 100 employees — may offer more limited investment options.

There is a positive trend among firms offering 401(k) plans toward providing increasing numbers of investment options. If your employer still offers limited choices that you feel are insufficient to allow you to invest as you wish, bring this to the attention of the plan administrators. It may be that you are not alone in wanting greater choice, and your employer may be persuaded to expand the options.

Keep in mind, however, that increasing the range of options adds to administrative costs and reduces the pool of money being invested in each particular fund. This, in turn, may increase average trading expenses. Particularly if you work for a small firm, these costs may not be worth incurring for your employer.

Remember

Whether you work for a large firm that offers numerous options or a small firm that offers only a few, you still have the opportunity to choose the classes of assets in which you want to invest and the risks you want to incur. This choice is advantageous both because it enables you to more closely tailor the available investments to you own needs and because it enables you to diversify your assets by investing through different funds.

Pre-retirement Withdrawal and Loans

Although not legally obligated to offer loans or hardship withdrawals, at least 85 percent of firms do include these options. Not surprisingly, many individuals are much more comfortable tying up a large part of their savings in a 401(k) plan if they can access these funds in some way in a time of need.

Chapter 9 discusses the details of loans and hardship withdrawals. But keep in mind that, within general guidelines set by the law, your employer has broad discretion when setting up a plan with regard to establishing under what circumstances one may be eligible, what interest rate will be charged on loans, and so forth.

Keeping Track of Employer Features

To help you keep track of what features your employer offers, you can use the checklist in Table 8-3.

Table 8-3: Checklist of Employer Offered Features

Option	Offered? (Y/N)	Notes
Matching contributions		How much_____
Eligibility requirements		Time on job_____ Age_____ For matching contributions?_____
Vesting rules		Type of vesting_____ Special rules_____
Valuation		Frequency_____
Investment options		Options offered: 1._____ 2._____ 3._____ 4._____
Hardships withdrawals		Eligible circumstances 1._____ 2._____
Loans		Eligible circumstances 1._____ 2._____

CHAPTER 9
ACCESSING YOUR SAVINGS BEFORE RETIREMENT

IN THIS CHAPTER:

- Loans on your 401(k) plan
- Hardship withdrawals before retirement
- Circumstances under which you won't face penalties
- What to do if you leave your employer
- Bankruptcy and divorce

When you contribute to your 401(k) plan, you are accepting strict limitations on spending your savings before retirement in exchange for the substantial tax benefits of 401(k) investing. Even in circumstances you feel justify withdrawing funds, you may face significant tax penalties. The law is intended to deter you from compromising your retirement savings for anything other than emergency expenses. So don't plan on using your 401(k) savings to take a trip to Tahiti, but if critical expenses do come up, the information in this chapter lets you know how to use your 401(k) savings to weather the storm.

Loans on the Value of Your 401(k) Plan

Your employer decides whether you can borrow against the value of your 401(k) account and under what circumstances you may do so. You are not required by law to demonstrate a pressing financial need in order to borrow. However, most plans do limit the circumstances under which you can borrow. The availability of loans is commonly limited to things like the following:

■ College tuition for you, your spouse, or your dependents

■ Uninsured medical expenses

■ Purchase of primary residence and payments necessary to prevent you from being evicted from your primary residence or from defaulting on your mortgage.

Table 9-1 lists and answers common questions about borrowing against the value of a 401(k) plan. To find out whether you can borrow for a particular need, check your Summary Plan Description or talk to your plan administrator.

Table 9-1: All about Loans on your 401(k) Plan

Question	Answer
What is the process of borrowing from yourself?	You may be able to simply request a loan verbally, or your employer may require a formal application.
	There is no credit check, and you cannot be turned down (as long as you have sufficient money in your account and meet the eligibility requirements).
	You are required to repay the loan, including interest, according to the agreed terms.
What is the interest rate?	The interest rate is typically the prime rate plus 1-2%.
What's the repayment schedule	Most loans have a repayment schedule of five years or fewer, although a large loan for the purchase of a residence may have a term of as long as 25 years.

How much can you borrow?	Half the value of your account or $50,000, whichever is less.
What if you default on a loan?	Defaulting on a loan is considered an unauthorized withdrawal and is reported to the IRS. As a result, you will immediately owe income tax plus a 10 percent penalty (unless you are over 59 ½)on the outstanding balance of the loan.
What if you quit or lose your job before paying the loan back?	If you are fired or quit, the balance of the loan may be immediately due and, if you cannot pay, will be reported as a withdrawal with the same tax consequences as for a default.

Warning

Borrowing from your 401(k) account can jeopardize your retirement plans. Do so only if you have no good alternative source of credit.

Is borrowing from your 401(k) account a good idea? The answer to this question depends very much on your alternatives. If you borrow from your 401(k) account and stop contributing new funds into the account while you repay your loan, you will certainly reduce your retirement savings substantially. However, if the money you are borrowing is necessary to meet a pressing need, and your best alternative method of financing would be at an interest rate much higher than the return you can expect to receive on 401(k) investments, then borrowing from your account is probably the best option.

Figure 9-1 shows how the value of an account over 35 years for three people (A, B, and C):

■ Individual A invests $4,000 every year.

■ Individual B takes a $15,000 loan in year 15, repays it over 5 years at 8 percent interest, and continues to contribute $4,000 annually to her account in addition to making loan payments.

■ Individual C takes out an identical loan, but stops contributing additional funds to her account during the five years of loan repayment.

Figure 9-1: Suspending contributions while you repay a loan to yourself seriously hurts your accumulated savings.

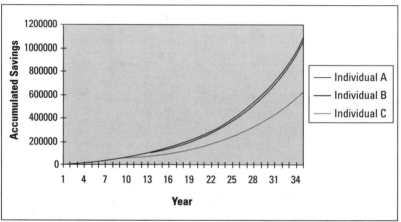

If you borrow from against the value of your 401(k) account, continue to make contributions as you repay the loan. Otherwise, you will greatly reduce your accumulated savings.

Hardship Withdrawals

As the name implies, *hardship withdrawals* involve simply withdrawing funds from your 401(k) account. These types of withdrawals are allowed only under circumstances that constitute a "hardship," described in the next section. Keep the following facts in mind about hardship withdrawals:

■ The IRS sets guidelines concerning when hardship withdrawals *may* be permitted, but your employer is under no obligation to permit them at all and can set greater restrictions than those the IRS imposes.

■ When you take a hardship withdrawal, expect nearly half of the amount you withdraw to be lost to taxes. Table 9-2 shows how much a hardship withdrawal could potentially cost you. (Note that the tax rates and penalties you would face depend on your state of residence and income tax bracket.)

Table 9-2:   Taxes and Penalties on Withdrawals

Event	Amount
Amount of hardship withdrawal	$10,000
Federal Income tax at 28%	-$2,800
Federal tax penalty of 10%	-$1,000
State income tax of 4%	-$400
State tax penalty of 2%	-$200
Amount you receive after taxes and penalties	$5,600

The IRS rules governing hardship withdrawals are constructed to greatly deter you from withdrawing money from your 401(k) plan unless absolutely necessary. Before you withdraw money from your 401(k), first consider taking a loan out on a value of your 401(k) account. (**Note:** If your employer uses the safe harbor rules, you have to borrow all you can first, and only then will you be eligible for a hardship withdrawal. See the section "What constitutes a hardship?" for information about the safe harbor rules.)

If you make a hardship withdrawal, you face income taxes and usually a 10 percent penalty tax, plus you can't replace the money in your account. Your retirement savings may never recover.

What constitutes a hardship?

The IRS rules governing withdrawals from 401(k) plans specify that a plan may permit a hardship withdrawal only if either of the following is true:

■ You face an immediate and heavy financial need

■ A withdrawal from the 401(k) plan is necessary to satisfy the financial need.

Clearly these basic guidelines leave some room for differing interpretations. Your employer can make determinations about eligibility for hardship withdrawals in one of two ways:

■ *The facts and circumstances test:* Your employer examines the facts and circumstances surrounding the withdrawal request and makes a judgment as to whether they meet the two requirements.

■ *The IRS safe harbor guidelines.* These guidelines specify that only certain circumstances satisfy the requirement of immediate and heavy financial need.

Many employers use the safe harbor guidelines. Table 9-3 lists the circumstances and conditions that safe harbor rules specify. To find out which test your employer uses, ask your plan administrator.

Table 9-3: Safe Harbor Rules and Conditions

Accepted Reasons for Withdrawal	Conditions of Withdrawal
Uninsured medical expenses for you, your spouse, or your dependents	The amount withdrawn cannot exceed the amount you need

Accepted Reasons for Withdrawal	Conditions of Withdrawal
Costs of purchasing your principal residence (this does *not* include mortgage payments)	You must have exhausted all other possible distributions (such as withdrawing any funds contributed after-tax) and available loans
Payment of college tuition, related fees, and room and board for the next 12 months for you, your spouse, or dependents	You are prohibited from making any elective contributions to the 401(k) plan for 12 months after the withdrawal
Payments necessary to prevent you from being evicted from your home or having the bank foreclose on your mortgage.	The amount you are permitted to contribute in the calendar year after the withdrawal is reduced.

When the 10 percent penalty doesn't apply

The IRS considers a few circumstances sufficiently dire that the 10 percent penalty tax is not applied to a hardship withdrawal:

- ■ You face unreimbursed medical expenses in excess of 7.5 percent of your income.

- ■ You are completely disabled.

- ■ The court has ordered that funds from your account go to a former spouse or dependent (called a Qualified Domestic Relations Order).

- ■ You leave your employer or are fired, and you are at least 55 years old.

- ■ You leave your employer, are *under* age 59 ½, and choose a section 72(t) withdrawal (described in the following section).

■ You've died and the money is transferred to your beneficiary.

Even though you don't have to pay a 10 percent penalty, you still owe income tax on the withdrawal.

Leaving Your Employer

If you leave your employer, you have several options to choose from that enable you to either continue investing your money for retirement on a tax-deferred basis (usually the best idea) or have immediate access to your funds. Table 9-4 lists the options available to you.

Table 9-4:   Options When Leaving Your Employer

Option	Description	Recommend For
Leave your saving with your former employer's 401(k) plan	Usually an option if you have a balance of at least $5,000. You can no longer contribute to the plan, but you will continue to earn tax-deferred returns on your investments.	Those who need time to decide where they want their money, like to a new employer's 401(k) when they take a new job.
Take a hardship withdrawal	You owe income tax on the full amount, plus you will owe a 10 percent federal penalty for early withdrawal (unless you are over 55).	Not recommended
Transfer your savings into your new employer's 401(k) plan	Known as a *rollover*. Make sure your new plan allows such transfers and find out whether you are immediately eligible upon employment. Also request a direct *trustee to trustee* transfer. See the following section for details.	Those who are going to a new job that offers a 401(k) plan

(continued)

Table 9-4: Options When Leaving Your Employer *(continued)*

Option	Description	Recommend For
Transfer your savings to an IRA.	You continue to earn tax-deferred returns and avoid any immediate tax liability; If you choose this option, open a new IRA, known as a *conduit IRA*. Do not transfer these savings into an existing IRA; otherwise, you won't be able to later roll it back into a 401(k) plan if you wish to do so.	Those whose new employer does not offer a 401(k), or who are not immediately beginning new employment.
Elect for *72(t)* Distributions	You receive the funds in your 401(k) account as periodic distributions based on IRS calculations of your life expectancy. If you choose this option you are locked into it for at least five years or until you reach age 59½, whichever is longer..	Those who need to begin receiving distributions. Consult with a financial planner to determine how much you will actually receive each year and how it will affect your retirement savings.

If you leave your employer, carefully consider what to do with the money in your 401(k) account. If you aren't careful, you could face a hefty tax bill that you might otherwise have avoided.

Rollovers

A *rollover* describes the transfer of funds from one tax-advantaged retirement vehicle — a 401(k) plan, IRA, 403(b), pension, and so on — into another in order to avoid taxes that would result if you simply withdrew the funds.

- Generally you are able to rollover funds in your 401(k) only if your employment ends, you become disabled, or you retire.

- The surviving spouse of an individual who died with money in a 401(k) plan can rollover the money only into an IRA.

You can execute a rollover in one of the following two ways: through a *direct rollover* or through a *regular rollover.* Table 9-5 explains each type of rollover.

Table 9-5:   Direct versus Regular Rollover

Direct	Regular
The trustee sends a check directly to the trustee of the new qualified retirement plan you're investing in; the money is never in your hands	You receive a check for the amount of your balance minus a 20 percent withholding by law.
Also called *trustee-to-trustee* transfer	
No required withholiding	20 percent required withholding; balance treated as a taxible distribution subject to income tax and 10 percemt penalty if you are under 55

(continued)

Table 9-5: Direct versus Regular Rollover (continued)

Direct	Regular
No exposure to tax	To be exempt from tax, must deposit money in a qualified retirement plan within 60 days

Always use a direct trustee-to-trustee rollover to avoid tax withholding.

You can rollover all funds in your 401(k) except for the following:

- Any contributions you made after tax (although these do not face taxes or penalties upon withdrawal anyway)

- Money you've borrowed from your 401(k) and not yet paid back

Bankruptcy and Divorce

If you declare bankruptcy, your creditors cannot seize the money you've saved in your my 401(k) plan. Federal law prohibits it. In this way, a 401(k) plan offers some protection for your retirement savings against a period of severe financial trouble.

Unlike creditors, your spouse or dependents may be able claim some of the money in your 401(k) account in the event of divorce. In order to do so, they have to get a *Qualified Domestic Relations Order* from the court, just as with alimony or child support. In the absence of such an order, only you can make decisions concerning your account.

Remember

The money you put into your 401(k) plan is earmarked for retirement, and you will face tough rules and potentially stiff penalties if you seek to use it for another purpose. Nevertheless, you should not feel that, in the event of a real financial emergency such as disabling injury or medical problems in your family, you cannot draw on your 401(k) savings. In order to encourage participation in 401(k) plans, many employers are loosening restrictions on borrowing from 401(k) accounts so employees feel less wary about depositing their money in the plan. This added flexibility is a good thing so long as you are careful not to dip into your retirement savings unnecessarily.

CHAPTER 10

RECEIVING DISTRIBUTIONS WHEN YOU RETIRE

IN THIS CHAPTER:

- ■ When you can and when you must begin distributions
- ■ Distribution options
- ■ What happens to your money when you die

When it comes time for you to retire and start reaping the benefits of your 401(k) savings, you still have some important choices to make. Should you start withdrawing funds as soon as you retire, or should you wait a few years if you can afford to? Should you withdraw your savings in one lump sum, take it in installments, rollover the money into an IRA, or buy an annuity? This chapter explains the options you have and helps you make informed choices that suit your retirement needs.

Deciding When to Start Receiving Distributions

The longer you can go without tapping into your retirement savings, the more comfortably you will be able to spend when you do retire. Of course, if you have saved and invested effectively and accumulated a substantial retirement nest-egg, you may want to buy yourself an early retirement. The decision is between a long retirement and a shorter but more luxurious one.

The graph in Figure 10-1 shows how delaying retirement can increase your assets and allow you to spend more each year after you retire. The example shows the effects of delaying retirement five years (from 65 to 70) for a person who has accumulated a total of $800,000, will live to be 90, and will take equal annual distributions. Retiring at age 65 allows annual spending of $69,250. Delaying retirement to age 70 allows annual spending of $110,500.

Figure 10-1:   The effect of delaying retirement from age 65 to 70.

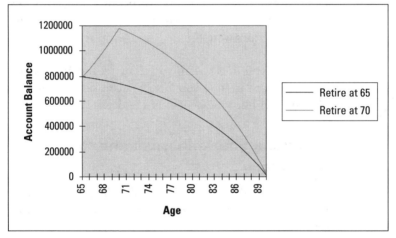

Working a couple of extra years instead of retiring can make a big difference in how well you can live when you do retire.

When you can begin receiving distributions

Of course, even if you could afford to do so, you can't retire at age 45 and begin taking money from your 401(k) account without penalty. You have to be at least 59 ½ years old to receive distributions without paying the 10 percent penalty for early withdrawals. When you receive distributions, you owe income taxes on those distributions (remember, 401(k) plans are tax-deferred, not tax-exempt).

Remember

You don't have to be retired to begin receiving distributions. Many people become "semi-retired" and work part-time and use distributions as supplementary income.

When you must begin receiving distributions

If you are retired and turn 70 before July 1 in a given year, you must begin distributions by April 1 of the following year. If you retire after age 70, you must begin distributions by April 1 following the year in which you retire. (Nobody said that the IRS's rules were simple.)

Remember

Even though you must begin withdrawing the money, you don't have to spend it. If you like, you can simply re-invest it, although without the benefit of tax-deferment.

Calculating your minimum annual distributions

You can use one of two methods to calculate your minimum annual distributions: the *term-certain* method and the *recalculation* method.

In the term certain method, your minimum annual distribution is based on your life expectancy (as determined by the IRS) when you begin distributions (or the combined life expectancy of you and your beneficiary, if applicable). To figure out what percentage of your total balance you have to receive annually, the IRS divides your balance by the number of years of your life expectancy. Then it multiplies this percentage by your total account balance at the start of each year (see Table 10-1).

Table 10-1: Example Calculation of Minimum Distribution

Item	Explanation
Age at which you begin distributions	65
Spouse's age	65
IRS estimated life expectancy	25 years
Minimum annual distribution in first year	1/25 (4%) of account balance at start of the year
Minimum annual distribution in second year	1/24 (4.16%) of account balance at start of the year

Estimated life expectancy is based on IRS actuarial tables (IRS Publication 939).

In the recalculation method, your minimum annual distribution is still based on the estimates of your life expectancy; however, each year, you recalculate your life expectancy according to the IRS's actuarial tables and re-compute your minimum required payment.

- In this method, the minimum distribution declines gradually year after year.

- If either you or your beneficiary dies, minimum distributions are recalculated rather than being locked into the original schedule. If this happens, you — or your spouse — may end up with suddenly increased distributions.

If you want to withdraw as little as possible from your 401(k) account each year, consult a financial planner to determine which method is best for you.

Warning

If you fail to receive the minimum distribution required by the IRS, you get hit with a 50 percent penalty tax (that's right, 50 percent) on the amount that you should have gotten but didn't.

Deciding How to Receive Distributions

When you retire, you have quite a few choices regarding what to do with the money you've accumulated in your 401(k) account:

- Do nothing. Leave your money in your 401(k) plan.

- Receive all your money as one lump sum distribution.

- Receive periodic installment distributions.

- Rollover your money into an IRA.

- Use your money to buy an annuity.

To help you decide among your options, the advantages and disadvantages of your alternatives are summarize in Table 10-2. For more information, see the following sections.

Table 10-2: Distribution Options

	Advantages	Disadvantages
Leave money in 401(k)	Simplest option	Must begin distributions after age 70½
	Continue earning tax-deferred returns	May take time to access your money
Take lump sum distribution	It's your money to do with as you please	You face a large immediate tax liability and no longer earn tax-deferred returns
Take periodic installments	Steady income stream	May be difficult to change distribution schedule once begun
	Lower tax bill than lump sum	
	Continued tax-deferred returns on invested funds	If you aren't careful, income stream may expire before you do
Rollover to IRA	Continued tax-deferred returns	A little more complicated than leaving your money in your 401(k) account for your former employer to administer
	Easier access than 401(k) account	
	More investment options than 401(k) plans	
Purchase an annuity	Can provide a guaranteed income for life	Offers a poor return on your investment

Leave the money in your 401(k) plan

Leaving the money in your 401(k) plan is an attractive option if

■ You haven't yet reached the age that distributions are mandatory (70 ½)

■ You don't yet need the money to live on

■ You are happy with the investment options your 401(k) plan allows

■ You want you money to go on earning a good return

Your money continues earning tax-deferred returns, and you face no tax liability until you withdraw it.

Some plans limit the ability of participants to leave funds in their 401(k) account after retirement. Also, you may not be able to make a withdrawal at will (moving money out of your 401(k) account can take a little time once you decide to do so), so be sure that you have sufficient funds to meet your short term needs.

Receive all your money as a lump sum distribution

Once you retire, there is nothing to stop you from taking all the money out of your 401(k) account. However, if you do, you face a substantial tax bill. Receiving all this income in one year usually means that most of it is taxed at a very high marginal income tax rate.

In the past, the IRS allowed five-year averaging so that if, for example, you withdrew a lump sum of $1,000,000, you could pay tax as though you were receiving $200,000 in each of the next five years. Doing so substantially reduced the tax liability, even though the entire tax bill was still due the year of the distribution. However, 1999 is the last year in which five-year averaging is permitted. If you were born before January 1, 1936, you are still eligible for ten-year averaging (even better than five-year average, but the same basic principle), but everyone else is out of luck.

Receive your money in periodic installment distributions

Most plans let you receive periodic distributions from your account in whatever amount that you want.

■ This strategy provides a steady stream of income while allowing the remaining balance of your account to continue earning tax-deferred returns.

■ You pay income tax only on the amount you receive each year.

■ The marginal tax rate you face on these distributions will probably be much smaller than if you received the money as a lump sum.

If you will rely on the stream of distributions for financial support, keep the following in mind:

■ Be careful that you allow for the possibility that you will live longer than you expect. If you are 65 and plan to receive distributions over twenty years, be sure that you set some of the money you receive aside in case you live beyond age 85.

■ Changing your distribution schedule or taking out extra funds for a one-time major purchase may be difficult once you start installment distributions.

Tip

Be sure you know and are comfortable with your plan's rules governing periodic distributions.

Rollover your money into an IRA

If you want to continue earning tax-deferred returns and face no immediate tax liability, you may want to consider rolling over your 401(k) money into an IRA.

■ An IRA gives you continued tax-deferred returns while providing easier access and more investment choices than a 401(k) plan typically does.

■ You face the same mandatory minimum distributions from an IRA as you do from a 401(k) account.

Purchase an annuity

An annuity is a contract with an insurance company to provide you (and possibly a joint beneficiary) an income for life and a death benefit. Many different types of annuities are available, but typically you (as the *annuitant)* are guaranteed a fixed stream of income payments either for as long as you live or for a fixed period. If you die early, your beneficiary may or may not receive remaining principal, depending on the type of annuity.

The guaranteed income of an annuity comes at a cost. You would likely have more to spend if you invest your own money, such as through an IRA, and are careful not to withdraw it too quickly.

If your greatest concern is guaranteeing income security for yourself or your spouse, an annuity may be an option worth considering. You should consult a financial advisor.

Upon your Death

What happens to your 401(k) funds when you die depends on whether you are receiving distributions at the time. See Table 10-3.

Table 10-3: 401(k) Plans and Death

Situation	Option
You've been receiving periodic installment payments and die while you still have a balance in your 401(k) account.	Your beneficiary can continue receiving distributions on the same schedule you had been.
You die before beginning to receive distributions.	Non-spouse beneficiary can receive money as a lump sum or spread withdrawals over five years.
Spouse beneficiary may have the option of spreading out withdrawals based on life expectancy.	

These options depend on the rules of your plan. Also, your beneficiary will owe taxes on all distributions he or she receives from your 401(k) account, just as you would have.

Bottom line: Think carefully and study your options before deciding what to do with your 401(k) account savings when you retire. Some decisions, such as taking a lump sum distribution, are irreversible and others, such as purchasing an annuity, can only be reversed by paying a significant fee. Your savings needs to last you for twenty or perhaps thirty years of retirement, so plan accordingly.

CLIFFSNOTES REVIEW

Use this CliffsNotes Review to practice what you've learned in this book and to build your confidence in doing the job right the first time. After you work through the review questions, the problem-solving exercises, and the fun and useful practice projects, you're well on your way to achieving your goal of investing in a 401(k) plan.

Q&A

1. What does it mean that a 401(K) plan is a *defined contribution* plan? What factors affect the benefit you will receive upon retirement?

2. What is the *primary* reason for investing your retirement savings through your 401(k) plan?

    a. Simplicity of participation

    b. Professional management of invested funds

    c. Tax deferment

    d. Ability to access funds prior to retirement in emergency

3. Match each of the following to an appropriate example of risk exposure: inflation risk, market risk, and specific risk.

    a. You invest a large share of your savings in the stock of the firm you work for

    b. The real purchasing power of your pension upon retirement may be much less the present value of the promised benefit

    c. Your savings is invested primarily in an index fund that tracks the Standard and Poor's 500 index

4. Approximately how much should you expect to receive annually from Social Security during your retirement (in today's dollars)?

    a. Less than $10,000

    b. $10,000 to $15,000

    c. More than $15,000

5. True or False: Employer matching of contributions doesn't help you much because these contributions aren't tax-deferred.

6. What does it mean when your 401(k) account is fully vested?

7. What do you owe if you take a hardship withdrawal from your account?

   a. Income tax on the amount of the withdrawal
   b. A 10 percent federal penalty tax
   c. Up to 2 percent state penalty tax
   d. All of the above

8. If you leave your employer for a new job and want to rollover your savings into your new employer's 401(k) plan, you should use a direct trustee-to-trustee rollover. Why?

9. What is the latest you can begin receiving distributions from your 401(k) account if you retire at age 65?

10. List two options for disposing of your savings at retirement that allow you to continue earning tax-deferred returns.

11. Which of the following should you consider when deciding how to allocate funds in your 401(k) plan:

   a. Stage of life
   b. Your personal tolerance for risk
   c. Your total wealth
   d. All of the above

Answers: 1. You choose how much to put into your account and are not promised any specific benefit upon retirement. Instead, your retirement income depends on your contributions and the returns on your investments. 2. c. Tax deferment is the primary reason, although the others are also true of 401(k) plans. 3. a. specific risk; b. inflation risk; c. market risk. 4. b. 5. False. 6. All contributions made into your account by your employer are legally yours. 7. d. This is true except in a few cases, such as complete disablement. 8. With a direct rollover, you avoid IRS withholding and possible tax liability. 9. April 1 of the year after you turn 70 ½. 10. Leave your money in your 401(k) and take installment distributions; rollover your money into an IRA. 11. D. All of the above.

Scenarios

1. Suppose your goal is to have $1,000,000 when you retire, you are forty years from retirement, and you currently have $5,000 in savings. Assuming a 10 percent annual return and using the tables in Chapter 4, calculate how much you need to save annually to reach your goal.

2. Using the same scenario as in the preceding, recalculate the amount you need to save annually if you have only thirty years until retirement.

Answers: 1. You need to save $1,588.60 annually. 2. You need to save $5,524.20 annually.

Practice Projects

1. Using the information in Chapter 7, design an appropriate investment portfolio for your stage of life and the level of risk you want to incur.

2. Use the information in Chapter 4 to determine what annual contribution you would have to make to generate a retirement income equal to your income today. Try the calculations with an aggressive investment strategy and a conservative one to see the difference it makes.

CLIFFSNOTES RESOURCE CENTER

The learning doesn't need to stop here. CliffsNotes Resource Center shows you the best of the best — links to the best information in print and online about investing and retirement planning. And don't think that this is all we've prepared for you; we've put all kinds of pertinent information at www.cliffsnotes.com. Look for these terrific resources at your favorite bookstore or local library and on the Internet. When you're online, make your first stop www.cliffsnotes.com where you'll find more incredibly useful information about investing and retirement planning.

Books

This CliffsNotes book is one of many great books about personal finance and investing published by IDG Books Worldwide, Inc. So if you want some great next-step books, check out these other publications:

- **CliffsNotes Planning Your Retirement,** by Michael Perry and Howard Sorkin. If you'd like to know more about planning and investing for retirement through additional means than your 401(k) plan, this is the place to look. IDG Books Worldwide, Inc., $8.99.

- **CliffsNotes Investing in the Stock Market,** by Edward Gilpatric. If you want to take a more active role in choosing the stocks you invest in, whether through your 401(k) plan or not, this is for you. IDG Books Worldwide, Inc., $8.99.

- **Investing For Dummies,** by Eric Tyson. For a more in-depth discussion of the full range of investment possibilities open to you, from real-estate to venture capital, this is a great source of information. IDG Books Worldwide, Inc., $19.99.

■ **Personal Finance For Dummies,** by Eric Tyson. With the help of this book you can learn to manage your money efficiently, reduce your debts, and save more of your income. IDG Books Worldwide, Inc., $19.99.

It's easy to find books published by IDG Books Worldwide Inc. and other publishers. You'll find them in your favorite bookstores (on the Internet and at a store near you). We also have three Web sites that you can use to read about all the books we publish:

■ www.cliffsnotes.com

■ www.dummies.com

■ www.idgbooks.com

Internet

Check out these Web sites for more information about investing and retirement planning:

■ **American Association of Individual Investors,** **www.aaii.com** — This is a great place to start learning more about investing. The site has links to many other investment sites. Access to parts of the site is limited to members of the association.

■ **Morningstar, www.morningstar.net** — This site is an excellent place to research mutual funds and find those that are best for you. It also has a 401(k) calculator to easily calculate how much you will have when you retire based on information about your contributions, expected returns, and so on.

■ **The Internal Revenue Service, www.irs.gov** — This is the easiest way to access IRS publications, including those on treatment of retirement savings.

- **The Social Security Administration, www.ssa.gov** — If you want to learn more about how your Social Security benefit will be determined or request an estimate of your benefit upon retirement, go to this site.

Next time you're on the Internet, don't forget to drop by www.cliffsnotes.com. We have created an online Resource Center that you can use today, tomorrow, and beyond.

Software

These programs can help you estimate retirement expenses, Social Security benefits, account for inflation, and project what you need to save to meet your retirement needs. They can also assist in planning your asset portfolio and researching funds.

- **Quicken Financial Planner.** Price: $40.00.
- **Microsoft Money Deluxe 2000.** Price: $69.95

Send Us Your Favorite Tips

In your quest for learning, have you ever experienced that sublime moment when you figure out a trick that saves time or trouble? Perhaps you realized you were taking ten steps to accomplish something that could have taken two. Or you found a little-known workaround that gets great results. If you've discovered a useful tip that helped you invest your money more effectively and you'd like to share it, the CliffsNotes staff would love to hear from you. Go to our Web site at www.cliffsnotes.com and click the Talk to Us button. If we select your tip, we may publish it as part of CliffsNotes Daily, our exciting, free e-mail newsletter. To find out more or to subscribe to a newsletter, go to www.cliffsnotes.com on the Web.

INDEX

403(b) plans, 61
72(t) distributions, 98

A

administration. See plan management
age
    maximum to begin distributions, 104
    minimum for penalty-free distribution, 103
    plan eligibility, 83
American Association of Individual Investors, 116
annuities, 110

B

bankruptcy, 100
beneficiary, 99, 110, 111

C

cash or deferred arrangement (CODA), 8
changing employers. See also leaving employers
    rollover, 97, 99, 100
    vesting policy, 83, 84
compound interest, 64
contributions
    annual cap, 11, 49
    annual goal calculation, 39, 40, 41, 42, 45, 46
    annual goal shortcoming, 49
    automatic withdrawal, 20
    employer matching, 81, 82
    limits, 11, 49
    voluntary nature, 11
corporate bonds, 54
cost-of-living adjustments (COLAs)
    Social Security, 12
credit cards, 33, 34

D

death, 99, 110, 111
debt
    credit cards, 33, 34
    liabilities worksheet, 24, 25

delaying retirement, 103
distributions. See withdrawal
diversification, 66, 67, 68
divorce, 95, 100

E

employee participation. See also contributions
    eligibility requirements, 83
    hardship withdrawals, 20
    investment choices, 19
    loans on 401(k) account, 20
    management involvement, 11
    vesting, 20
    voluntary nature, 11
employer involvement
    hardship withdrawal policy, 93, 94
    investment options offered, 85, 86
    loan policy, 89
    matching contributions, 81, 82
    plan management, 20
    plan offering, 10
    valuation policy, 85
    vesting policy, 83, 84
equities
    common stocks, 55, 57
    equity mutual funds, 51, 56
    risk, 55, 65

F

financial self-assessment
    calculating expenses, 27
    debt, 33
    financial obligations, 29, 30, 31, 32, 33, 34
    net saving, 26, 27, 29
    net worth, 23, 24, 25
    savings goals, 31
    unexpected events, 31, 32
fired, 95
flexibility, 19, 20

G

government bonds, 53
guaranteed investment contracts (GICs), 54, 55

W

CliffsNotes™

Your shortcut to
SUCCESS™
for over 40 years

Computers and Software
Confused by computers? Struggling with software? Let *CliffsNotes* **get you up to speed on the fundamentals —** **quickly and easily. Titles include:**

Balancing Your Checkbook with Quicken®
Buying Your First PC
Creating a Dynamite PowerPoint® 2000 Presentation
Making Windows® 98 Work for You
Setting up a Windows® 98 Home Network
Upgrading and Repairing Your PC
Using Your First PC
Using Your First iMac™
Writing Your First Computer Program

The Internet
Intrigued by the Internet? Puzzled about life online?
Let *CliffsNotes* **show you how to get started with e-mail,** **Web surfing, and more. Titles include:**

Buying and Selling on eBay®
Creating Web Pages with HTML
Creating Your First Web Page
Exploring the Internet with Yahoo!®
Finding a Job on the Web
Getting on the Internet
Going Online with AOL®
Shopping Online Safely